Brushes & Bayonets

In association with

OSPREY
PUBLISHING

THE ILLUSTRATED
LONDON NEWS
PICTURE LIBRARY

Brushes & Bayonets

Cartoons, Sketches and
Paintings of World War I

LUCINDA GOSLING

First published in Great Britain in 2008 by Osprey Publishing,
Midland House, West Way, Botley, Oxford OX2 0PH, United Kingdom.
443 Park Avenue South, New York, NY 10016, USA.
Email: info@ospreypublishing.com

A CIP catalogue record for this book is available from the British Library.

ISBN: 978 1 84603 095 6

Page layout by Myriam Bell
Index by Alison Worthington
Typeset in Centaur, Harrington and Bernhard Modern
Originated by PDQ Digital Media Solutions Ltd.
Printed in China through Bookbuilders

08 09 10 11 12   10 9 8 7 6 5 4 3 2

For a catalogue of all books published by Osprey please contact:

NORTH AMERICA
Osprey Direct c/o Random House Distribution Center
400 Hahn Road, Westminster, MD 21157, USA
E-mail: info@ospreydirect.com

ALL OTHER REGIONS
Osprey Direct UK, P.O. Box 140, Wellingborough, Northants, NN8 2FA, UK
E-mail: info@ospreydirect.co.uk

www.ospreypublishing.com

Front cover: 'What's all this about unmarried men', Bruce Bairnsfather, *The Bystander*, 5 January 1916.
Back cover: 'Sunshine and Dust near Neuville St. Vaast – A scene on the British Lines of Communication',
Edward Handley-Read, *The Sphere*, 31 August 1918.
Title page: 'The Long and the Short of It', Bruce Bairnsfather, *The Bystander*, 30 August 1916.

Contents

Dedication

This book is dedicated to the memory of my mother, Pamela.

Acknowledgements

My sincere thanks to Marcelle Adamson, Katie Simpson, Annalaura Palma and Sophie Basilevitch at The Illustrated London News Picture Library, who coped with urgent research requests and a deluge of picture scans with patience, efficiency and good humour. I would also like to acknowledge the help of Terry Parker, who provided useful information on a number of artists' lives. I am grateful to Jim Davies for his knowledge of Fortunino Matania and to Simon and Majorie Watts for information on their late father, Arthur Watts. Amanda-Jane Doran, during her time working with me at the ILN Picture Library, ignited my latent interest in the illustrators of the early 20th century, which I thank her for. Professor Gary Sheffield kindly read through the text and offered a number of useful suggestions and improvements. Ruth Sheppard at Osprey Publishing first saw the potential in the holdings of The Illustrated London News archive and asked me to write this book. I thank her for her help, support, unfailing enthusiasm and unswerving belief in the project. Finally, I would like to thank my family, friends and work colleagues who put up with my World War I-dominated world during the writing of this book and offered endless encouragement during the final Big Push.

An Illustrators' War

Introduction

On 31 March 1915, a drawing appeared in *The Bystander* magazine. The half-page black and white illustration depicted a trembling assortment of British Tommies, bunched close together in a makeshift shelter, saucer-like eyes betraying their alarm at a shell exploding vigorously overhead. It was entitled, 'Where Did That One Go?' and it was to launch its author on a career that would transform him into one of the best-loved personalities of the Great War. *The Bystander* also added a subtitle:

A Sketch from the Front — A reproduction of a sketch sent home to us from the Front of an officer of the 1st Royal Warwicks. 'I have drawn it', he writes, 'as well as I can under somewhat difficult circumstances, and, I may say, from first-hand impressions.'

That officer was Captain Bruce Bairnsfather, 1st Battalion, Royal Warwickshire Regiment, as he was duly credited in his next published picture when it appeared in *The Bystander* on the 21st of the following month. In terms of war illustration, the publication of 'Where Did That One Go?' is a significant landmark. Bairnsfather, through his association with *The Bystander*, would become a global celebrity, and the most popular artist of the Great War. His cartoons of the trenches and their grumpy inhabitants, who bore the deplorable conditions with cynical fortitude, were the perfect antidote to the gloom, prompting General Sir Ian Hamilton, the Commander-in-Chief of Home Forces and later the Mediterranean Expeditionary Force, to dub Bairnsfather, 'the man who won the war'. There can be no greater accolade for an artist of that period.

As it was, Bairnsfather's pairing with *The Bystander* was purely coincidental. After training as an artist he had seen limited success as a commercial artist, then had worked as an electrical engineer before the outbreak of war. But the sketching bug caught up with him when he was in France. Drawing relaxed him, as it did many soldiers who, in the endless hours spent in the trenches, had little to amuse them and welcomed any pleasurable distraction. Bairnsfather's sketches, with their bittersweet blend of world-weariness and dry humour, began to gain popularity in the trenches, and he was commissioned by a number of officers who desired to decorate their dug-outs with Bairnsfather's cartoons. Eventually, a fellow subaltern suggested he send his pictures to one of the illustrated papers for publication. As it happened, a copy of *The Bystander* was lying around and, noting that its size and shape matched that of his drawing, he selected it to be the recipient of his sketch. Nobody was more surprised than Bairnsfather when, a few weeks later, he received a letter of acceptance from the editorial offices of *The Bystander* at Tallis House in The Strand, London, together with a cheque for two guineas and a request for further drawings.

Launched in 1901, *The Bystander* was a successful weekly magazine specialising in art, literature, sport, motoring, theatre, gossip and political comment. It was regarded as one of the finer quality magazines, and its long run of 39 years (1901 until 1940 when it merged with *The Tatler*) is testament

to its popularity. *The Bystander* was witty and urbane, appealing to a sophisticated and fairly well-heeled readership. Today, it is one of the nine publications that form *The Illustrated London News* archive. *The Bystander* now shares shelf-space with *The Tatler* and *The Sketch*, both magazines with broadly similar content. However, they did not become stablemates until 1927, when, under the title of 'The Great Eight', the three magazines, along with their older, more sober siblings – *The Illustrated London News*, *The Graphic* and *The Sphere* – plus *The Illustrated Sporting and Dramatic News* and *Britannia & Eve*, amalgamated and moved to the imposing premises of Inveresk House, at the junction of the Aldwych and Strand in London. Back in 1914, the magazines were friendly rivals, chasing the same stories and jostling for position on the newsstands. *The Bystander* was originally allied to *The Graphic*; *The Tatler* was an offshoot of *The Sphere*; and *The Sketch* was the younger, livelier sister of *The Illustrated London News*, one of the grand old titles of Fleet Street.

Launched on 14 May 1842, *The Illustrated London News* can lay claim to be the world's first illustrated newspaper. Its founder, Herbert Ingram, had the then revolutionary notion of producing a weekly publication filled with pictures of events and people, while the news was still current. He engaged the finest artists and engravers who worked round the clock on woodblocks, which would eventually appear as beautifully realised impressions upon the printed page. Hard as it is to imagine today, the 'ILN' was a sensation, and its intelligent mix of news reporting and entertaining features ensured its place as one of the most respected and revered publications of the last two centuries.

The *ILN*'s strong tradition of illustration set a benchmark for future publications, and it seemed only natural that eight journals with only the highest standards of artistry would eventually join forces. The *ILN* fought off many impersonators over the years, and it is ironic that perhaps its most prestigious opponent, *The Graphic*, set up by William Luson Thomas – previously an engraver with the *ILN* – should eventually become part of The Great Eight.

'A Sketch from the Front: Where Did That One Go?', Bruce Bairnsfather, *The Bystander*, 31 March 1915

Between them, the magazines of The Great Eight launched the careers of some of Britain's best-loved illustrators and artists. The *ILN* originally courted established artists, with Ingram securing the services of Sir John Gilbert for its first and many subsequent editions, but a number of illustration's great names owe their career to one or other of the *ILN* magazines. Bairnsfather is one; William Heath Robinson is another, admitting in his autobiography, *My Line of Life*, that Bruce Ingram's decision to publish him in *The Sketch* in 1905 'fairly launched me on my career as a humorous artist'. Both artists – Bairnsfather in *The Bystander* and, during World War I, Heath Robinson in *The Sketch* – increased the popularity and the circulation of their respective publications. Bairnsfather, restricted by a contract with *The Bystander*, rarely had his work published anywhere else.

Most illustrators were ordinary men with an extraordinary talent, although the majority had honed their raw skills at one of the famous art schools in London – Heatherley's, Frank Calderon's, The Press Art School, or the New

School of Art set up by John Hassall and later re-named The London and New Art School when Hassall joined forces with Frank Brangwyn. They continued to learn even once they had achieved recognition. A great number of the illustrators in this book belonged to the London Sketch Club. It was a social club, but members would still meet each week to produce a sketch within one hour, afterwards comparing notes and offering advice to one another. They moved in the same circles, and many came from artistic families. George and Edwin Morrow had no fewer than six other brothers, four of whom were artists. Heath Robinson and Charles Robinson's father had been an engraver for the *ILN* and *Penny Illustrated*, and their eldest brother Thomas also worked as an illustrator. The work of both Reginald and Ralph Cleaver was published in *The Bystander* and *The Graphic*, while brothers H. M. and C. E. Brock shared the same studio.

Possessing talent was not always enough to guarantee success and illustrators' chosen career required them to work hard and to sell themselves. Fledgling illustrators would be expected to hawk their work around Fleet Street until they found an art editor in sympathy with their style or humour, and as most had families to support, it was essential they ensured a constant flow of commissions. While a percentage of illustrators might achieve substantial financial reward as well as artistic fame, others struggled, finding that despite plentiful work, their lack of business acumen was a disadvantage. Bairnsfather did not benefit from his cartoons as much as *The Bystander*, which owned the copyright and controlled all licensing of his work. His earnings regularly seemed disproportionate to the popularity of his cartoons. The emergence of artists' agents around this time usually guaranteed a steady stream of work; Francis & Mills and A. E. Johnson were the biggest and allowed illustrators to concentrate on their art, while their agents handled the

'He Draws the Pictures – and the Crowd', unknown artist, *The Bystander*, 24 May 1916
Crowds gathered before the windows of *The Graphic* Gallery at 190, Strand, where the Bairnsfather War Pictures were on exhibition.

business side of things. Few artists ever considered any type of commission 'beneath them'. As well as the plethora of illustrated magazines in circulation, most would undertake advertising commissions, poster work, designs for postcards and china, brochures and, of course, illustrations for the lavish children's books found in all the best nurseries. It is hardly surprising that the latter end of the 19th century and the early part of the 20th was known as illustration's 'golden age'.

The advent of war did little to diminish such a fertile period, and although paper shortages and censorship presented many challenges to the press, the high-quality illustrated magazines weathered the storm well. The enormous proliferation and extraordinary diversity of pictures produced in magazines at this time is in itself impressive, but it is the unconscious revelation of detail that is most fascinating, and which forms the fabric of the Great War story. *Colour* magazine, a monthly periodical covering the contemporary world of art and illustration, observed a change in artistic focus in July 1916:

> *Art, in spite of adverse conditions is showing much vigour and the ability to render service in many directions. Since the war began there has been a notable movement to bring art into closer touch with everyday affairs, even of the humblest description.*

In many ways, illustrators (as opposed to 'fine' artists) had always had the common touch, and their work during the Great War period continues to offer us a glimpse into everyday lives. Steering well clear of the high-minded, the cerebral or the indulgent, illustration puts flesh on the bones of history. Sometimes the jokes can be anachronistic, but they tell us what people were feeling and thinking. After all, illustrators were part of a collective voice and firmly echoed popular opinion. In comparison to the war poets, the propaganda posters or the canvases produced by official war artists such as Paul Nash or C. R. W. Nevinson, 'illustration' has been woefully neglected

Advertisement for John Hassall Correspondence Art School, *The Bystander,* 17 January 1917 (the successor to The London and New Art School)

The Bystander. November 8, 1916.—No. 675. Vol. LII

The BYSTANDER

TO FRANCE FOR "FRAGMENTS"

Captain Bruce Bairnsfather on his return to France after short leave in England. He will, should his duties permit, continue to supply the readers of "The Bystander" at home and abroad with food for laughter by means of his inimitable representations of life at the Front—some of which may shortly take a novel turn

as a resource – a great pity considering the hundreds of thousands of people who would have read at least one illustrated magazine each week. In an age without the web, television or even radio broadcasting, newspapers and magazines were a lifeline and an essential part of life. The beauty of illustration was that, in the hands of the talented, it could capture a moment or a mood without the need for wordy explanations. An empathy with the man in the street (or the man in the trench) and a skill at translating this shared experience onto paper was the essence of the illustrator's work.

No mainstream newspaper or magazine ever questioned the overall justness of the war, but as the conflict progressed, there were opportunities to gently criticise, poke fun or even incite controversial opinion. Wily magazine editors knew that they must feed their readers. Some clamoured for the sentimental or jingoistic; others had darker, wittier tastes. Whatever was needed, the illustrators gave it and the public lapped it up.

Illustration had for many years lived a comfortable existence alongside photography, over which it continued to have many advantages, particularly in wartime. It was certainly difficult for either illustrators or photographers to be present during actual offensives, but illustrators would draw from eyewitness accounts given after the event, and could juxtapose figures to make a more satisfying composition, adding to the overall clarity of a picture. Flick through any copy of *The Illustrated London News* from this period, and it is impossible not to be struck by the unexpected superiority of the illustrations over photographs. Fortunino Matania, renowned for the intricate detail and accuracy of his war pictures, visited the Front on several occasions. To bolster his research, he was known to visit wounded soldiers in hospital, taking with him toy soldiers to use as props. A one-man production line of World War I illustrations, Matania churned out accomplished pictures of pinpoint accuracy, some of which would become part of World War I folklore.

'To France for "Fragments"', *The Bystander* front cover, 8 November 1916

Illustrators from this period can roughly be divided into two camps – those who drew scenes and events from the war, either from eyewitness information or first-hand experience, and those who mixed humour, metaphor or caricature to show a lighter side of the war. The former appeared predominantly in the more serious titles, while the latter fit well with the values of the younger magazines. I hesitate to give these illustrations the wholesale description of cartoons – some were simply humorous drawings or appealing colour plates with witty captions. There is a third group – that of the soldier-artist; amateur artists at the Front who sent in their sketches. *The Bystander* in particular regularly encouraged men at the Front to send in their work, a practice that must have enhanced its patriotic kudos.

It is not altogether surprising that there was a copy of *The Bystander* on hand in the incongruous setting of the trench inhabited by the Royal Warwickshires, 'somewhere in France'. The magazines were keen to advertise their popularity, if not indispensability, to Tommy at the Front. Allowing for an element of self-publicity, their argument was nevertheless supported by genuine letters praising the morale-boosting effects of favourite publications, and by several photographs of soldiers shown smiling together over a shared magazine. Indeed, for its 22 December 1915 issue front cover, *The Tatler* printed a photograph of four gunners perched on the wheels of their gun, engrossed in the Christmas issue. The magazines also implored readers to donate their spare copies to the war effort. *The Sketch* ran a header:

Send Your 'Sketch' to the fighting-men. This paper may be handed in over the counter of any Post Office – without packing, address, or postage. It will then be sent either to our sailors or to soldiers at the Front.

Meanwhile, *The Tatler* printed a letter on its cover from an anonymous soldier, touching in its politeness:

I do hope you will forgive the liberty I take in addressing this appeal to you, but I have on one or two occasions had the great pleasure of seeing your book, The Tatler... I have wondered if one of your very generous readers would care to send me their copy after they have finished with it. It does not matter how old or dirty it may be so long

The Tatler front cover photograph, 'We are Fed Up with News – Send Us "*The Tatler*"', 22 December 1915

as the inside is there. I would not trouble you, but my folk at home are not in a position to send it. . .It would do your eyes some good if you could only see our boys crowding around the one book, and on some occasions, it may be only a few pages someone has found. I expect some lucky officer had it sent to him. . .

The last sentence is perhaps a reference to *The Tatler*'s usual reader. The illustrated magazine market was roughly divided into the higher quality 'sixpenny weeklies' such as *The Sketch* and *The Graphic*, while at the cheaper end of the market were the 'two penny weeklies', including *London Opinion*, *John Bull* and *The Passing Show*. *The Tatler* rose above them all by adding an extra penny, charging 7d. by the end of the war, and thereby restricting its readership to the upper classes. As the boys in the trenches clearly saw no reason why they could not share the delights of a 7d. magazine, it would have done *The Tatler* no harm to show an altruistic side.

One of the greatest (and most popular) artists of the World War I period is Raphael Kirchner, whose 'Kirchner Girls', the forerunner of the pin-up, were published exclusively in Britain by *The Sketch*. Just as *The Bystander* promoted Bairnsfather, so *The Sketch* did Kirchner, and it is fascinating to see photographs published in the magazine showing dug-outs whose walls are brightened by the soft, feminine outlines of Kirchner's beauties. In November 1915, a page was devoted to six poems written by a group of men whose main topic of conversation was a Kirchner work pinned to the wall of their shared dug-out, 'the only piece of femininity among six males'. One poem, short and sweet, indicates the power of illustration on a soldier starved of any female company:

The Married Man

When I turned about in the small dug-out,
My glance on the picture tarried;
So I hied me away from the fair display,
Remembering I was married.

The Sketch produced regular portfolios of Kirchner's work. They proved hugely popular, prompting the magazine to run a full-page announcement headed 'BEWARE!' warning their readers that the only way to guarantee getting a copy containing Kirchner's painting was to subscribe. It was a thinly disguised marketing ploy, but probably with some substance, considering Kirchner prints are still in demand with collectors today.

The Bystander, having complete exclusivity on Bruce Bairnsfather's work, was not backward in commercially exploiting it either. It produced portfolios of his 'Fragments from France' postcards, and, recognising Bairnsfather's photogenic looks (he had soft eyes and good bone structure), regularly printed photographs of the captain in France or at work in his studio. The famous French artist, Marcel Poncin, was even commissioned by the magazine to draw Bairnsfather in a French lingerie store, an illustration that no doubt might have embarrassed the mild-mannered Bairnsfather. *The Bystander* also organised a series of lectures, which Bairnsfather dutifully undertook, much to the detriment of his health (he was recuperating in hospital with shellshock when his first picture was published and would suffer from exhaustion and nervous incidents for the rest of his life). His avuncular creation, 'Old Bill', became the subject of several successful stage revues, plays and films, pottery lines and car mascots. Bairnsfather was *The Bystander*'s 'golden goose'. Vivian Carter, editor of *The Bystander*, even allocated a member of his staff to manage Bairnsfather's affairs and to act as his agent.

Bairnsfather had trained at John Hassall's School of Art in Kensington, West London. Hassall, with his bold lines and flat colour, remains one of the most notable illustrators of the 20th century. During the war, advertisements for his school appeared regularly in magazines, encouraging soldiers to send him their work for a no-obligation professional opinion. Percy Bradshaw, who ran The Press Art School (and published monographs of contemporary artists and their work), placed advertisements for his school emphasising the usefulness of drawing skills for soldiers – both for practical purposes and for leisure. The advertisements serve to highlight the popularity of illustration at all levels and explain, to a certain extent, the star status of Britain's favourite artists.

While magazines were keen to publish work by amateur soldier-artists, there were many professional artists serving in the forces. Bruce Bairnsfather's humour drew on genuine experience, as did that of naval men Sub-Lieutenant Arthur Watts and Lieutenant E. G. O. Beuttler, whose work features in this book. Watts gained the DSO, while E. H. Shepard (of *Winnie the Pooh* fame)

'The Artist – Then – And Now', Howard K. Elcock, *The Bystander*, 13 June 1917

won the Military Cross during the Third Battle of Ypres. Lawson Wood, another hugely successful comic artist, was a balloon observer for the Royal Flying Corps and was decorated by the French. Lionel Edwards, the equestrian and sporting artist, served as an officer in the Army Remount Service. Countless other artists joined up, many with the Artists' Rifles, an elite Territorial regiment with roots dating back to 1860 and whose early members included the Pre-Raphaelite Brotherhood. The regiment consisted mainly of writers, actors and artists. The illustrators Harold Earnshaw, Bert Thomas, James Thorpe, Edward Handley Read, W. B. Wollen and Fred Buchanan all joined 'the Artists" during World War I, as did the poet Wilfred Owen. Bruce Ingram, grandson of Herbert and editor of *The Illustrated London News* and *The Sketch*, was a lieutenant in the East Kent Yeomanry when war broke out. He joined the Royal Garrison Artillery in France as a captain, won the Military Cross in 1917, was awarded the OBE (military, 1918) and was mentioned three times in despatches. There were tragedies too. H. H. Munro, who wrote for *The Bystander* under the pen-name 'Saki', enlisted in the 2nd King Edward's Horse despite being over age. He transferred to the 22nd Royal Fusiliers but was shot in the head in No Man's Land on 14 November 1916. The artist Philip Dadd was killed the same year.

There were others who did not see action. Some, like Heath Robinson, who was 42 at the outbreak of war, were too old, while both H. M. Bateman and George Studdy felt bitterly disappointed that their health prevented them from joining up, although the latter served in the Voluntary Aid Detachment (VAD) for some of the war. All three artists arguably contributed more to the war effort by staying put at their easels.

'Not Very United Artists!', H. M. Bateman, *The Sketch*, 7 October 1914

Caption: *Our Artist Writes: I understand that members of the artistic professions are forming a corps of their very own. Everyone will admire their patriotism; but is there not fear that their very originality and desire to be able to be unlike others in any way will be their undoing? I have imagined a sergeant has just given the order 'Left turn!'*

(© H. M. Bateman Designs Limited/ILN Picture Library)

They also contributed some of the funniest images of this book, the aim of which is not to offer a complete, comprehensive history of World War I, but instead to tell the story of this unique period in history through illustrators' eyes. It is a tribute to the artists working for a specific, but influential, group of magazines, who combined personal talent with a keen perception of the public mood. For anyone discovering these illustrations for the first time, they are a link with a powerfully emotive past, reaching far beyond the constraints of dry textbook facts.

The selection is often personal; of pictures that made me laugh, smile or simply wonder. They are taken from an archive that is so impressive in its depth, breadth and variety, it would be impossible to attempt to include everything in one book. The number of battle and action scenes alone is staggering and could fill several volumes, yet can only be represented by a modest number of pictures here. My choices have followed the twists and turns of the magazines themselves, and I have allowed certain themes to predominate when the quantity and quality of the illustrations suggest they were the preoccupying topics of the time – at least for the readers of these magazines. The same applies to the balance of work by specific artists, including Heath Robinson, Bairnsfather, Matania and Kirchner, who all remain popular today, and for good reason.

There is, unapologetically, a bias towards the humourous, light-hearted material which, in many ways, seems to capture the spirit of the magazines and perhaps the spirit of the people who read them. How much of this was the manifestation of avoidance humour can only be guessed at, but comedy in the face of adversity appears to be the British way. This sentiment was expressed succinctly in *The Tatler* in April 1917 with regard to the illustrations of 'Rilette':

> *The 'Rilette' paintings to the commission of H. Dennis Bradley are deliberately light in atmosphere. The tragedy of war we all realise. It needs no illustration.*

Some of the most enduringly famous images of the war originated from one or other of the *ILN* magazines. A number of these are included but it is 90 years since the majority of these pictures were last published. About half of the artists have disappeared into obscurity, and I remain staggered at how such talent can be so easily forgotten. Of the remainder, only a small number are still familiar today, the rest known only to collectors, experts and enthusiasts. Despite their obscurity, they have their part to play in telling the story of World War I and it is a joy to be able to give their work prominence once more.

My hope is that this collection gives you as much pleasure as it gave to me, and to the millions who enjoyed the pictures nine decades ago. Illustration deserves a place alongside the poetry and fine art of World War I. It is the heritage of the Great War laid out in ink, pen and pencil.

'Over by Christmas'

The Outbreak of War

It is a commonly acknowledged fact that war sells newspapers. In view of this, there is an inherent expectation, when browsing the bound volumes of magazines in *The Illustrated London News* archive, that the assassination of the heir to the Austro-Hungarian throne and the unfolding crisis of July 1914 would be front-page news. Not so. War took Britain entirely by surprise, and by default, the British press, who only managed to recognise the looming significance of the events in Europe days before Britain herself declared war on Germany. With the benefit of hindsight, this apparent state of blissful ignorance appears staggeringly insensitive. But it does serve to highlight the fact that Britain had no intention – or indeed interest – in involving herself in what was considered, in those crucial weeks, a Balkan squabble.

While Britons basked in the long, hot summer days of 1914, there was no inkling of the cataclysm that was about to be unleashed when Serbian student Gavrilo Princep aimed his gun at Archduke Franz Ferdinand and his wife in Sarajevo. Princep not only committed murder, but triggered a chain of events that would lead to a conflict of such magnitude and destruction, it was far beyond most people's imagination.

As Austria-Hungary and Serbia traded increasingly belligerent ultimatums and counter-ultimatums, as Russia mobilised her armies in Serbia's defence,

as the German generals dusted down the plan of Count von Schlieffen, and as France prepared to support her Russian ally, Britain casually observed a burgeoning crisis, which remained a sideshow to more pressing domestic events, specifically the Irish Home Rule question that dominated the press during July. The 'Tragedy of Serajevo' (sic) warranted a modest four-photograph spread in *The Illustrated London News* on 14 July, yet far more pages were given over to the recently deceased politician Joseph Chamberlain. And with no small

---

'The Little Contemptibles: Autumn 1914 – Fighting in the Open Country Before Trench Warfare', W. B. Wollen, *The Sphere*, 4 January 1919

In the weeks preceding the establishment of trench warfare, described by *The Sphere* as 'a heroic period full of epic deeds', the opposing sides fought in open countryside, finding vaguely adequate shelter where they could, in this case a low grass ridge. The infantry here are using rifles to stem the onrush of German troops, exploiting the skilful regulars who were able to fire 'fifteen rounds rapid' from the superior British Lee-Enfield rifle. Certainly German accounts of this period show that the British rifle fire was sometimes mistaken for that of machine guns.

amount of irony, the same issue also carried a double-page illustration of English sailors giving a boxing demonstration (the latest craze in 1914) to their German 'confreres' on HMS *Ajax* at Kiel. More naval interest followed in the next issue, which was devoted to the King's inspection of the fleet at Spithead. *The Graphic* also dedicated many pages to this display of Britain's naval might, both papers blissfully unaware that within a matter of days, the fleet would be called upon to put their training and manoeuvres into practice.

One might expect some recognition of the anxious state of affairs in the following week, but instead the *ILN*'s 25 July issue seemed gripped by the sensational Caillaux murder case in France, and numerous advertisements for Thomas Cook and the railway companies suggested European seaside resorts and spas as suitable destinations for the forthcoming Bank Holiday weekend. *The Graphic* printed photographs of women's and children's fashion from Berlin.

By 1 August, the *ILN* had acknowledged that this was 'The Greatest War Cloud That has Hung Over Europe since 1870'. Yet curiously, in a report accompanying photographs of Berlin gripped by 'war fever', the crowds of German demonstrators marching through the street were heard to shout, 'Hoch, England!' as they passed the British Embassy. Even then, a war where Germany and Britain were enemies seemed improbable to most.

Finally, on 8 August, four days after Britain declared war on Germany, the press suddenly shook itself awake. Frederic de Haenen, one of the *ILN*'s 'special artists', produced a somewhat murky halftone illustration of crowds outside Buckingham Palace; Steven Spurrier drew German nationals leaving Liverpool Street station for *The Graphic*; while Fortunino Matania pictured a similar scene for *The Sphere*. *The Graphic* found it necessary to place an advertisement in its own paper:

'THE OUTBREAK OF WAR'
Owing to the crisis, we have decided to suspend Mr Arnold Bennett's Articles, 'From the Log of Velsa' and 'ILLUSTRATE THE WAR' in the completest way by Photographic Records & Drawings. 'The Graphic' Artists & Representatives (Like our Sailors & Soldiers) Have Been Mobilised.

The Sphere's 8 August issue conceded that events had overtaken them:

Since the previous issue of The Sphere was published, events have marched with extraordinary rapidity, and the war cloud which appeared on the south-eastern horizon of Europe has now spread into one vast canopy until it overshadows the whole of the Continent and the British Isles.

The media were not alone; the population as a whole was taken by surprise. Albert Kinross, writing in *The Graphic*, spoke of how the news of war finally permeated the quiet Kent village where he lived, the main preoccupations of which at that time of year were 'hops, cricket and the fruit crop':

Till Friday July 31st, we were unconscious of anything unusual; then, only then, did the better-instructed among us begin to take the prospect of war with any seriousness.

The declaration of war prompted an immediate volte-face among the *ILN* magazines. To use *The Graphic*'s terminology, they mobilised into action, deploying correspondents abroad and sweeping away anything that might be regarded as trivial. The major players, the maps, the soldiers, the uniforms and soon the first confrontations suddenly displaced all other news. It was only a matter of weeks before advertisers began to use military images, and as early as 19 August, *The Illustrated London News* had launched its own spin-off entirely dedicated to the war, *The Illustrated War News – A Pictorial History of the Great War*. More poignantly, the first Roll of Honour was published in *The Graphic* on 12 September 1914.

As well as reportage-style illustrations by artists such as H. W. Koekkoek and A. Van Anrooy in *The Graphic*, Frederic de Haenen and Frederic Villiers in *The Illustrated London News*, and Fortunino Matania in *The Sphere*, humorous artists soon got to work. The mood in the first few months of the war was one of unalloyed optimism, served up with a dollop of righteousness as to the cause Britain was fighting for. It was generally believed that the war would be over by Christmas. Young men – petrified not of what they might face on the battlefield, but that the whole thing would be over before they stood on French soil – were anxious to join up as soon as possible. Lord Kitchener was almost a lone voice when he told a surprised Cabinet that he predicted the war would last at least three years and Britain would need to raise an army on a continental scale to meet its challenges.

'Crowds cheering the King & Queen outside Buckingham Palace following the declaration of war', Frederic de Haenen, *The Illustrated London News*, 8 August 1914
As the deadline of the British ultimatum to Germany drew closer, crowds began to gather outside Downing Street and the gates of Buckingham Palace. King George V noted in his diary, 'Tuesday August 4. I held a Council at 10.45 to declare war on Germany. It is a terrible catastrophe, but it is not our fault. An enormous crowd collected outside the Palace; we went on the balcony both before and after dinner.' The mood of the crowd, which according to the *ILN* 'sang the National Anthem with the utmost fervour,' was celebratory.

'Britannia Bides Her Time', Alick P. F. Ritchie, *The Bystander* front cover, 19 August 1914
In 1914, Britannia really did rule the waves, and it was widely expected that the outcome of any forthcoming conflict would be decided at sea. But like so many aspects of the war, the reality did not comply with expectations. An editorial in *The Graphic* confirmed British confidence in her naval superiority, commenting on the absence of incident in the early weeks as, '…a very striking tribute to the adequacy and efficacy of the British navy…At any instant we must be prepared to hear of a desperate dash of the German ships to sea – desperate because we hold the ocean with such superiority that, barring miracles, the defeat and the annihilation of the German navy is a foregone conclusion.' A profile of Ritchie in *The Strand* magazine likened his style to 'sly travesties of the cubists, the Futurists, and other eccentric products of the modern movement' and his 'Puck-like gift of freakishness' resulted in a variety of satirical styles.

'To Arms, Britons! Avert These Horrors: The Triumph of Science and Efficiency',
Frank Reynolds, *The Sketch*, 2 September 1914

A typical propagandist reminder to the British of what they were fighting for, this brutish
German soldier, half-human, half-ogre, trampling innocent Belgian women and children
underfoot, pulls no punches, although its savageness is unusual for *The Sketch*. The caption asks,
'*Would you like the same things to happen here? Would you like to see your mother and sisters killed or maltreated,
your property destroyed and your homes burnt? If not – those of you who are eligible – answer Lord Kitchener's
call to arms, and join the ranks. If you cannot join the active army or the Territorial, do anything else you can.*'
The atrocities committed in Belgium by the invading German army did much to galvanise
public opinion and to encourage British men to join up, although the monstrous image here
is in stark contrast to the rather harmless-looking Germans depicted opposite.

'The Armageddon Reservists Leaving London', Fortunino Matania, *The Sphere*,
15 August 1914

This picture by Fortunino Matania shows German reservists leaving London from Victoria
station. They are destined for Queensborough in Kent, from where they would catch a boat
to Flushing, now Vlissingen in Holland. On 1 August, when Germany declared war on Russia,
there were 35,000 Germans living in Britain. Those who went to answer the call of their own
country often left wives and children in Britain; however, many preparing to leave Britain were
arrested and detained by police under the Aliens Restriction Act, hastily passed by Parliament
on 5 August. It stated that after 10 August, enemy aliens would be unable to leave the United
Kingdom without a special permit, leading to a huge exodus in the little time available. By late
September, 13,600 Germans and Austrians were in internment camps.

'With the British Regulars During the Famous Retreat From Mons – August 25, 1914', W. B. Wollen, *The Sphere*, 4 January 1919

The retreat from Mons, as suggested by the title of this painting by W. B. Wollen, became part of Great War mythology. It was the decision of General Joffre to fall back and to prepare for a counter-offensive. In 14 days, the French armies and British Expeditionary Force covered around 250 miles, with many battles fought against the pursuing Germans. Here, in the narrow streets of Landrecies, soldiers of the Grenadier, Coldstream and Irish Guards successfully repel a German attack. William Barnes Wollen was a sporting and military painter, who along with his *ILN* contemporary, R. Caton Woodville, specialised in the '*Boy's Own*', triumphalist style of war painting that appealed to popular taste.

'France and Britain Together in the Field: A Scene During the Fighting of the Autumn of 1914', Fortunino Matania, *The Sphere*, 1 February 1919

In 1919, *The Sphere* published a number of illustrations as a retrospective of the war's early months. This colour painting by Matania shows the aftermath of an early action in which the French and the British have dominated and taken German prisoners. A local priest acts as a Red Cross worker, while a French soldier tends to his wounds, and the British guard their German prisoners. The French soldier wears the navy 'kepi', jacket and voluminous bright red trousers that were the trademark of the French army. Deemed too conspicuous, the uniform was rapidly phased out after heavy French losses in 1914, despite protestations, and replaced with grey-blue (known as 'bleu d'horizon') in 1915. Likewise, the spiked 'Pickelhaube' helmet worn by the German soldiers was seen less and less as the war progressed.

'Why Don't They Get a Move On?', Ralph Cleaver, *The Bystander* front cover,
27 January 1915

'It'll be over by Christmas' was the phrase used by many in 1914. Most people's idea of war
was of a series of swift and valiant battles between mobile armies with a decisive conclusion.
There seemed to be no reason to believe that this war should be any different. This illustration
takes the opportunity to criticise the critics, those blustering armchair strategists who
expounded their outdated views on tactics from the comfort of club land, while brave soldiers
at the Front were learning to cope with the trials and hardships of new, industrialised warfare.

'The New Year – By An Optimist', George Studdy, *The Bystander*, **30 December 1914**

The mood is tongue in cheek, and yet there remains a hint of hopeful optimism in this cartoon
by George Studdy, who imagines the Kaiser imprisoned as a star exhibit at the British Museum
by the end of 1915, as well as underwater tourist excursions off the coast of East Anglia to
view the sunken German fleet. (© George Studdy/ILN Picture Library)

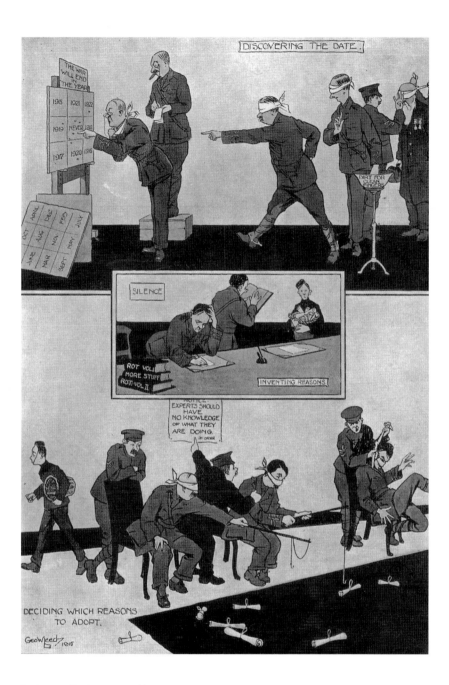

'When Will The War End?', George Weedy, *The Bystander*, 31 March 1915

Caption: *Military Experts Deciding When the War Will End and Why*

Following the realisation that the war had patently not been won by Christmas, speculation continued about when it might be over. George Weedy's rather biting cartoon in *The Bystander* emphasises the uselessness of prediction, but with these military experts relying on blindfolded conjecture, it is also a wry portrayal of a commonly held, but misguided belief that continues to this day – that senior military staff were clueless blunderers, detached from the reality of war.

'A.D. 19** (?)', Bruce Bairnsfather, *The Bystander*, 29 September 1915

Caption: *'I see the War Babies Battalion is a'comin' out'*

Bruce Bairnsfather depicts two veteran Tommies with Methuselah-like beards, still manning the trenches in an unspecified year sometime in the future; a light-hearted comment on the endless and frustrating stalemate of the Western Front.

'The Tatler Xmas Number', *The Tatler* Christmas Number, 2 December 1914
This bold design for *The Tatler*'s Christmas number front cover in 1914 exudes the confidence and optimism that characterised the first few months of the war. Sadly, the artist is not credited, although it could be Annie Fish, who also illustrated 'Letters from Eve' in *The Tatler*. It is a move away from the sentimental Edwardian-style narrative illustrations still employed by magazines such as *The Illustrated London News*, which preferred more literal and sentimental subjects for their Christmas covers – soldiers home on leave or families toasting absent fathers.

'A War Dictionary', Will Owen, *The Illustrated Sporting and Dramatic News*, 9 December 1916
Will Owen's lively, fluent style and genial humour guides readers through a number of new war-influenced expressions such as 'strafe' (punish) and 'blighty' (Britain) which, for a time, would become a daily part of Britain's lexicon. Some of the slang terms originating during the Great War are still used in the modern-day vernacular. Top-ranking staff officers were known as 'brass'; 'pipsqueak' was a small-calibre German shell; while 'dud' was a shell that failed to explode.

'War Nerves: Terrible Effect of a Clap of Thunder. A Result of Undigested War News: Is it a Zeppelin Bomb?', Tony Sarg, *The Sketch*, 12 August 1914

In the days following Britain's declaration of war, a nervous civilian population was consumed by overblown rumours of enemy spies and aerial raids. Tony Sarg's cartoon gently mocks these nervous Londoners' fear of a possible Zeppelin attack, unaware that a year later, the Zeppelins would indeed loom over the capital. Tony Sarg was an American who had been born in Guatemala. He moved to England in 1908 and his fascination with London, and especially the East End, is borne out by his cartoons, usually with 'Cockneyesque' captions. He also produced a number of posters for London Underground.

'How Some Englishmen – Thought We Were Going to Win the War', Thomas Maybank, *The Bystander*, 9 September 1914

Four sporting 'toffs' armed with nothing but their golf clubs and cricket bats holding up a charge of fierce German Uhlans may be an exaggeration, but for a generation fed on a diet of Victorian children's books full of gallantry and derring-do, there was an elementary belief that the British sense of fair play, as displayed on the cricket and rugby pitches of English public schools (as well as the country's 'business as usual' approach), would eventually win the day. One letter to *The Times*, from an officer at the Front on New Year's Day, 1915, makes liberal use of sporting terminology: 'There is a pretty good din going on all round, since our big howitzers are at present shelling the German trenches just in front of us and giving them absolute hell. They have been driven out of their trenches in places and as they spring across the open we bowl them over. Huge fun!'

'Who's for the Trench, Are You, My Laddie?'

Enlistment, Recruitment & Training

Even the briefest glance through any of the *ILN* magazines during the Great War reveals that illustrators were consciously part of a huge, nationwide recruitment drive. One of *The Bystander*'s regular contributors, Alfred Leete, was the artist behind the war's most iconic poster, from which Lord Kitchener's finger pointed mercilessly, announcing to the viewer, 'Your Country Needs You'. It was a message that was repeated countless times. In reference to Kitchener's career as a pin-up, Margot Asquith remarked of him, 'He is not a great man, he is a great poster', but in truth, Kitchener's achievement deserves more recognition. Lloyd George likened him to a lighthouse, with only periodic flashes of brilliance, but Kitchener's creation of the 'New Army' – a force of unprecedented size to meet the demands of a war of unprecedented scale – remains an unequalled contribution to the war effort. Without his foresight, the British Expeditionary Force of a mere 247,000 men would eventually have been overwhelmed by the German military. The plans Kitchener put in place in the first few months of the war without doubt laid the foundations for Britain's eventual success. For this, he deserves credit.

Out of a total of 5,700,000 British men who served during World War I, just under half of those had voluntarily enlisted, and a large number of those in the first two months of the war (3 September 1914 saw a staggering 33,204 men join up). Kitchener's campaign, which aimed to raise an army of 500,000, relied unequivocally on the support of the press, a challenge the *ILN* magazines appeared to take up with gusto.

Initially, any man aged between 18 and 31 could enlist, but following complaints in the press, the limit was soon raised to 35 for men without prior service, 45 for ex-soldiers and 50 for ex-senior NCOs. In order to join up, men had to pass a basic medical test which checked teeth, eyesight and chest measurements. In 1914, recruitment officers could afford to be choosy and some men discovered to their surprise that they were deemed unfit for

'Rank Outsiders', Charles Sykes, *The Bystander*, 2 September 1914
This double-page spread picture by Charles Sykes documents a scene drawn from life one week in late August 1914. While the Inns of Court Regiment drilled on the Embankment, scores of young men 'of military age and physique and in easy circumstances are content to look idly on, fully knowing that the call to the colours grows more urgent with every day's march of the enemy towards Paris'. The tone of moral disgust is palpable.

service. Both George Studdy, who had a lame foot due to an accident with a pitchfork in his youth, and H. M. Bateman, who suffered from rheumatic fever after a brief spell at the training camp of the London Regiment during the damp winter months, were declared unfit. Both men were bitterly disappointed, and in the atmosphere of public humiliation, in which civilians were treated as an inferior race, Bateman, often prone to depression, declared himself a 'hopeless dud'.

As Kitchener's Army continued to swell, it became clear that while there were a huge number of men ready to fight 'for King and Country', they were unable to do so due to lack of uniforms, weaponry, provisions and accommodation. Initial enthusiasm was soon followed by boredom and confusion. Many men had not been able to enlist in their battalions of choice, either because they were oversubscribed, or yet to be enlisted. Unable to slip instantly into khaki, many disappointed men had to make do with serge uniforms in 'Kitchener blue' until new supplies arrived.

Without proper equipment, and often housed in very spartan accommodation – sometimes in tents throughout their training even in winter – new recruits were then put through training aimed at toughening them up. This mainly consisted of monotonous 18-mile marches and constant drilling, sometimes with brooms, as supplies still lagged behind recruitment numbers. But it was the methods and techniques of training that raised scepticism. Men were taught to advance in an unwavering formation and obey orders at all costs. Little emphasis was placed on machine gun warfare and coverage of close, hand-to-hand fighting varied widely, an oversight that would have devastating repercussions on the battlefield. In the end, the battlefield was where the real lessons were learnt.

Despite the success of Kitchener's scheme, huge losses during 1915 meant that 700,000 volunteers would not be enough and indicated that a different kind of persuasion might be needed. The Derby scheme – a final attempt to sustain the voluntary principle of military enlistment – was introduced in October 1915 by Lord Derby, who already had a strong track record in recruitment, having raised five battalions of the King's Liverpool Regiment. The scheme called upon every man between the ages of 18 and 41 to 'attest' (to undertake to enlist when required to do so). The scheme also built on the foundations laid by Kitchener and continued to encourage men from the same office or factory to join up together in 'Pals' battalions, and offered a pension to any married men with dependents. These carrots were dangled along with a deadline of 15 December 1915 after which men who had not attested would risk conscription at a later date. In many ways, the scheme was inspired, appealing to the herd mentality and the enthusiasm men felt about joining up together, but it had limited success. Only 343,000 eligible men attested despite a special appeal by the King, and it turned out that the majority of them were married, leaving around one million bachelors still in civvies.

Public pressure, specifically from women, certainly played some part in persuading (or shaming) men to take the King's shilling. Baroness Orczy's Active Service League pledged 'to persuade every man I know to offer his services to the country', while the Order of the White Feather offered feathers to any young man found wearing civilian clothes. Poems and songs, especially those written by Jessie Pope in the *Daily Mail*, urged men to join up, or women to support their decision. In the light of such a coercive atmosphere, a number of illustrations tackle the awkward subject of identification for those who had hoped to join up but were rejected.

The efforts of Britain's female population were not sufficient to boost flagging recruitment numbers, and on 5 January 1916, Asquith introduced the Military Service Bill, which provided for the call-up of single men and childless widowers aged between 18 and 40. By March, it had extended to married men who had attested under the Derby scheme, and when this contingent complained that some unmarried men were still evading service, the National Union of Attested Married Men was formed to campaign for equality of sacrifice. Finally, April brought full-scale conscription for all men of military age but it was still not enough. Shortage of manpower was a persistent problem, and by 1918, the age limit had been raised to 51.

'Sketch Puzzle Picture: Find the Man Who Has Enlisted!', Frank Reynolds, *The Sketch*, 17 November 1915

This cover illustration by Frank Reynolds, published in *The Sketch* in the autumn of 1915, takes one of the most popular themes in recruitment propaganda – the contrast of the satisfaction and pride of a man who has enlisted, with the skulking shame of one who has not, while the recruitment posters plastering street walls in the background drive the message home. Frank Reynolds, best known as art editor of *Punch* after the war, was 38 years old when war broke out in 1914 and was consequently too old for traditional enlistment. But Reynolds was no preaching hypocrite. He served in a coast defence unit of the Cheshire Regiment early on in the war, and later in a section of the intelligence staff concerned with pictorial propaganda.

'Study in Still Life', Thomas Maybank, *The Bystander*, 6 January 1915

Women were valuable allies of the government when it came to encouraging men to enlist. Famous posters such as 'Women say "Go – Your Country Needs You…"', and organisations such as the Order of the White Feather tapped into feminine patriotism in a blatantly unsubtle fashion. Thomas Maybank prefers to offer a comic slant, with his two spinsters giving new meaning to a poster imploring 'Men Wanted' under which they unwittingly sit.

Above: 'Man Power in the Recruiting Office: A perfectly impartial method of dealing with doubtful cases', W. Heath Robinson, *The Sketch*, 30 January 1918
Right: 'Kultur: The Drilling-Machine for Military Beginners', W. Heath Robinson, *The Sketch*, 30 December 1914

Heath Robinson, the acclaimed 'gadget king', managed to dream up an appropriate piece of machinery for every aspect of the war, not least the recruiting office and the training ground. Enlistment and training often felt like being part of a rather random and elaborate production line, or perhaps like being trapped in a Heath Robinson drawing. While new recruits are literally wheeled in and then placed onto a human roulette wheel in one picture, 'military beginners' are rigged up to a convoluted series of cords and pulleys to speed them through basic drills in another. At the beginning of the war, the army, by and large, reflected class divides, with officers recruited from public schools and privates from the working classes. Nevertheless, some men who might have otherwise gained commissions chose to join the ranks, preferring to work their way up through merit and often to join up with friends, while those not traditionally regarded as "officer class" found the army was most likely to recognise their leadership qualities as the war progressed. One member of a unit in the Royal Fusiliers battalion describes the sleeping arrangements in a hut at the battalion's camp in Hornchurch, where the brother of a peer had one bed, and his former driver had the other. The three men in Heath Robinson's picture wear rather different clothes – one in a top hat, another in a flat cap – reflecting this burgeoning element of egalitarianism. (© Mrs J. C. Robinson by kind permission of the proprietor and Pollinger Limited/ILN Picture Library)

'What's all this about unmarried men?', Bruce Bairnsfather, *The Bystander*, 5 January 1916

By January 1916, manpower was becoming scarce, forcing the government to introduce conscription for all single men up to the age of 41. The minimum age was 18, but underage enlisters were fairly commonplace, particularly if they were bigger than average, in which case most recruiting officers would turn a blind eye. Bairnsfather's baby-faced new recruit might have had trouble meeting the minimum height requirement, although that in itself fluctuated throughout the war. When the war began, the army set a standard of 5 feet 3 inches, which was quickly raised to 5 feet 6 inches on 11 September 1914 to stem the flow of recruits. Two months later, when it became clear that the level of volunteers was fast diminishing, the original requirement was reinstated, and even special 'Bantam' units formed to take advantage of the surfeit of undersized men hoping to enlist. One correspondent from *The Times* very logically pointed out that smaller men had the advantage of being more difficult to hit, and only required shallow trenches!

'Single Men First!', Dudley Tennant, *The Bystander*, 12 January 1916

Caption: *'Aren't you sorry you jilted me now, Algy?'*

It has sometimes been suggested that the increase in marriages between 1915 and 1916 may have been influenced by the introduction of conscription for unmarried men. A continuing shortage of men resulted in an extension of conscription to married men later in the year, but for the time being, this young woman feels that her former fiancé has got his just deserts.

'The Marriage Tie', Arthur Watts, *The Bystander*, 2 December 1914
Arthur Watts uses quiet restraint to illustrate a man torn between duty to his country and duty to his family. The Derby scheme of autumn 1915 encouraged many married men to attest, but by April 1916, full-scale conscription meant that marriage offered no escape.

'"In the King's Name" – The Householder's Share in the War: "Billeting" Troops in an English Village', Lawson Wood, *The Illustrated War News*, 19 August 1914
Lord Kitchener's call for recruits in 1914 was met with an overwhelming response, and the question of persuading men to join up was soon displaced by the more mundane logistical problem of where to house the thousands of newly recruited soldiers during training. While some men put up with sleeping 12 to a tent, others might be lucky enough to be billeted in a home at a local village close to camp. Stays were usually short and the number of men to provide for varied between two and 50 depending on the size of the accommodation (higher numbers would be quartered at public houses, hotels or other large establishments). Householders were asked to provide accommodation free of charge where possible, although the army did authorise a scale of payments. Lodgings and attendance for a soldier with meals was scheduled at 9d. per night; breakfast, 7½ d., dinner, 1s. 7½d., and supper, 4½d. This is an unusual subject for Lawson Wood, who was a highly successful humorous artist. (© Estate of Lawson Wood/ILN Picture Library)

'Oh for the Touch of a Vanished Hand!', Wilmot Lunt, *The Tatler*, 9 September 1914

Caption: *Jimmy: 'The Germans won't 'arf cop it now. Farver's gone to Belgium and 'e's taken 'is strap wiv im'*

In the days when physical punishment for childish misbehaviour was universally accepted, this cheeky young chap feels confident that the presence of his disciplinarian father will soon frighten off the Germans. His optimistic attitude was one echoed by many on the Home Front. Paternal absence during the war was generally thought to contribute to juvenile delinquency, especially among children aged 11 to 13. Cases in the National Archives record an increase in the birching of boys ordered by the courts from 2,415 in 1914 to 5,210 in 1917.

'Daddy's Regiment', Lawson Wood, *The Illustrated Sporting and Dramatic News*, 14 November 1914

The war would change family life irrevocably. Many husbands and fathers who went to war came back as strangers, or with missing limbs. Some did not come back at all. Lawson Wood this time turns his hand to a moving subject, showing a small boy – his mother's protective arm around him – saluting bravely as his father's regiment marches past. Lawson Wood subtly depicts the passing soldiers as shadows cast by the afternoon sun as if to comment on the fleetingness of human life. The picture is a powerful one, highlighting not just the sacrifice of the men who went to fight, but also that of the families left at home. (© Estate of Lawson Wood/ILN Picture Library)

Above: 'The Great Army of "Armleteers" Marching To The Country's Call', Christopher Clark, *The Sphere* front cover, 18 December 1915

Right: 'Now Then, Lord Derby!', Dudley Tennant, *The Bystander*, 10 November 1915

Caption: *Why not carry the khaki badge idea further and put the label on the spot, so that the discarded might walk the streets with conscious rectitude?*
Lord Derby, organiser of the Derby scheme, announced publicly that, 'When the war is over I intend, as far as I possibly can, to employ nobody except men who have taken their duty at the front.' Many other employers took a similar stance,

and those who were declared unfit for service found themselves in the awkward position of having to explain their lack of uniform. Those who had attested under the Derby scheme were given armlets of dark khaki bearing a scarlet crown, as in this picture by Christopher Clark which featured on the front cover of *The Sphere* shortly after the scheme had closed. Dudley Tennant's cartoon suggests a similar device, advertising individual complaints and allowing rejected volunteers to walk with their heads held high.

'People We Don't Envy', G. E. Studdy, *The Bystander*, 27 January 1915

Caption: *No.II – The Army Service Subaltern compelled to deliver a lecture on Supplies to a contingent of men recruited from grocers, butchers, provision dealers, etc.*

The Army Service Corps (ASC) existed to arrange and supply all provisions to the combatant element of the army. Although sometimes derisively referred to as 'Ally Sloper's Cavalry' by the fighting infantry (after a comic strip character renowned for his evasive personality), some in the ASC ran significant risks, especially drivers, who were often required to travel well within range of the German artillery. Many members of the ASC were appropriately gleaned from the ranks of retailers and merchants, a fact not lost on this inexperienced, bashful officer, who is attempting to impart his flimsy knowledge of supply chains to a seasoned bunch of shopkeepers. Studdy's picture also underlines the regular disparity in age between commissioned officers, often as young as 19 or 20 years old, and the men they commanded.

A letter to *The Times* in 1916, in defence of quartermasters, complains that such men are not given the recognition they deserve, 'and who in this time of war have borne the brunt of the worry of mobilisation – too busy to make any effort at advancement – see boys of 19, 20, 21 come into their battalions...in six months or so are senior to the quartermaster, a man who possibly has served his grateful country for 20 or 30 years (possibly before that boy was born)'. (© George Studdy/ILN Picture Library)

'No Fear!', Charles Grave, *The Tatler*, 2 December 1914

Caption: *'Blowed if I'd risk my bloomin' neck!'*

Aircraft were introduced right at the beginning of the war as reconnaissance craft, but would still have been a rare sight in the skies. This curmudgeonly workman, disregarding his own precarious position, growls to himself that he wouldn't be foolish enough to take the risks of a pilot.

'The Latest "Lot" at Christie's', Charles Sykes, *The Bystander*, 23 September 1914

Caption: *The Auctioneer: 'Eton! Harrow! Marlboro'! going at one-and-tuppence – one-and-tuppence – going – gone! They go to the gentleman on my right – Lord Kitchener'*

The public schools of England had consistently supplied the Victorian and Edwardian armies with gentleman officers. By 1914, around 150 public schools and 20 universities had established their own Officer Training Corps, naturally prompting the War Office and the Admiralty to look to these institutions to provide officers with rudimentary training and leadership skills. Beyond these practical benefits, the public school system embodied and nurtured what were considered the ideal characteristics to lead men into battle: honesty, duty, sacrifice, strength and endurance – attributes that together formed the foundations of the concept of 'muscular Christianity'. Early in the war, many men of officer potential were unable to earn a commission unless they had been to a school with its own OTC; a situation experienced by R. C. Sherriff, author of *Journey's End*

who signed on initially as a private. He became captain in the 9th East Surrey Regiment from 1917, and won the Military Cross. Casualty rates were substantially higher among the officer classes than in the ranks and there is a sense of symbolic sacrifice in this picture by Charles Sykes.

'1914–1916 – War's Transmutations', Helen McKie, *The Bystander*, 27 November 1915

As a rule, officers were generally drawn from the upper classes, but there was still opportunity to progress through the ranks. As Helen McKie's picture suggests, in this meritocracy, an officer may find himself the superior of his former employer, or commanding men twice his age.

'The Shell and the Kernel of a Knut', William Barribal, *The Illustrated Sporting and Dramatic News*, 16 October 1914

The expression 'knut', now obsolete, was used to describe young men with dandyish pretensions, preoccupied with appearance and sybaritic pleasures. The transformation of a man from 'knut' to soldier, off to fight for a higher cause, was a potent symbol, contrasting the triviality of his previous existence with the honour and purpose of the new. Barribal painted another version of this image for a part-advertisement, part-recruitment poster, commissioned by Pope & Bradley (the men's tailors), substituting a silk top hat for the trilby, demonstrating how enthusiastically every part of the population was involved in the recruiting process.

'Our Costly Arms', unknown artist, *The Bystander*, 20 October 1915

Caption: *Recruiting Officer: 'Married and eleven children? Why hang it all man, you'll cost as much as the Colonel!'*

From 1 March 1915, separation allowances, the wage paid to men with dependents, increased to 12s 6d. for a man with a wife, and 21s for a man with a wife and two children, with 2 shillings extra for each additional child. For officers, and even many moderately well-paid middle class clerical and office workers, the pay offered by the War Office could sometimes be less than they had previously earned, showing that, for most, money was not a primary motive for joining up. Yet for the unemployed or manual workers, army wages were a welcome alternative to financial hardship, particularly for those with numerous offspring.

Frightfulness

Drawing the Enemy

Most illustrators love a villain and in the late summer of 1914, the Germans did not disappoint. Within a week of the war's outbreak, stories of German atrocities began to appear in the press. Even the *ILN*, usually fairly objective in its outlook, was quick to report on the barbaric Hun striding through Belgium leaving a trail of destruction and worse in his wake. Many stories were lurid and without truthful basis, fascinating to a public that had an almost vicarious appetite for subjects that were ordinarily taboo, although the readers of the *ILN* magazines were spared the most gruesome stories.

The Germans, similar in many ways to their British counterparts, had not always been the traditional enemy. Many Germans lived and worked in Britain, particularly in London and in seaside towns. Some had English spouses. There were strong marital bonds between the English and German royal families, and the Kaiser, eldest grandson of Queen Victoria, for the most part cut a strangely popular figure in the British press. But the photographs of him, dressed always in extravagant military uniform as 'All Highest War Lord' hint at a legacy of militarism going back to Otto von Bismarck and the Prussian position as the major power on mainland Europe after the 1870–71 Franco-Prussian War. Many late 19th-century commentators had predicted that a great war in the future was inevitable, although the potential aggressors varied depending on the fluctuating power shifts. France,

Russia, even China were sometimes cited as the enemy, but Germany's increasingly belligerent attitude during the early years of the 20th century, coupled with the paranoia surrounding the growth of her navy (stirred up by such Teutophobic newspapers as the *Daily Mail* or *National Review*) sowed the seeds of suspicion and ignited fears about how Britain would cope in the event of war.

The press viewed Germany's military professionalism with a certain degree of contempt. The British saw themselves as fair and square sportsmen. By

'Another Germ-Hun Authority: Father Christmas Captured by the Cohorts of "Kultur"', Lawson Wood, *The Tatler*, 2 December 1914
Lawson Wood caricatures the typical German soldier down to a tee in this picture, in which even Father Christmas (along with his reindeer and sleigh) is confiscated by the pompous and humourless 'Hun'. In reality, the Germans loved Christmas as much as any other Christian nation. The diary of a German lieutenant, Kurt Zemisch, even describes how the British cheered when the Germans illuminated their trenches with candles and a tree during the Christmas truce of 1914. (© Estate of Lawson Wood/ILN Picture Library)

preparing in advance, Germany simply wasn't playing the game. Later, Germany's embracing of 'total war', with unrestricted submarine warfare, Zeppelin attacks on civilians and the use of poison gas on the battlefield added further to Germany's barbaric and distinctly unsporting reputation. The British perception of valour, enshrined by the public school system and promulgated by patriotic magazines such as *Boy's Own*, was to die gallantly for one's country, often against the odds and according to the age-old code of chivalry. Germany's idea of war was to win it, at all costs, using any means necessary. Authors and journalists revelled slightly in the role of heroic underdog, confident that, in the spirit of Agincourt, righteousness and bravery would win the day, even if the reality was that British martial technology and the public's thirst for blood were regularly at odds with such a myth. And if Germany thought their version of 'total war' would cow the enemy, they were wrong. The sinking of the *Lusitania* in May 1915 and then the execution of British nurse Edith Cavell in October 1915 served only to fan the flames of British (and in the case of the former, American) outrage. By engaging in a modern, 'total' war, Germany in fact helped to whip up the Allies' patriotic fervour and strengthen their resolve.

What is significant is that there was far more vitriol and anti-German feeling from civilians on the home front than from the fighting men, who resented the media's libellous portrayal of 'Fritz' (privates tended to refer to the Germans as 'Fritz' or 'Jerry', whereas officers used the term 'Bosch' or 'Hun'). An extraordinary English children's book from the period, *The Red Book of the War*, edited by Herbert Strang, included a chapter entitled 'Germany – Enemy of the Human Race', instilling anti-German thoughts at an early age. Heath Robinson was an exception; he felt sympathy for the German POWs who worked occasionally in his garden, finding them to be 'simple and guileless'. He would 'accidentally' leave cocoa, bread and cheese in his garden shed whenever they were around, despite instructions not to feed them.

Soldiers at the Front also tended to take a more philosophical approach to the Germans. The Christmas truce of 1914 is of course legendary, but there were other instances that demonstrate a sort of jolly and gentlemanly acceptance of the enemy. One letter to *The Scotsman* in January 1915, from a British soldier, describes a dogfight involving one German aircraft against 16 French and British.

The soldier wrote, 'The German escaped unscathed and we gave him a great cheer for the odds were against him and he must have been a great chap.' It may be a rather odd and almost charitable view, but most British soldiers knew the stories circulating at home about the German troops being cowardly or physically inferior to be patently untrue, and such claims diminished their own achievements against what was a formidable enemy. One fabulously scathing piece in *The Bystander* from February 1915 under the heading, 'Mud, Blood and Khaki', written by 'An Officer on Leave', seeks to debunk the myths surrounding the Germans:

We are not, and of this I am more than assured, going to give the Germans a thrashing by belittling either their supplies, their courage or their numbers. Nor would it be paying ourselves a great compliment were we to 'crush' – to use a pet expression of the Press – a half-starved, cowardly enemy, numerically no stronger than our forces.

But ridicule remained a safer (and funnier) option for illustrators, whose portrayal of the enemy took many forms – dim, ponderous, cowardly, brutal, humourless, savage; the possibilities were endless. Interestingly, the Austrians and even the Turks were left alone almost entirely, the former perhaps lacking the cohesive national character of the Germans and the latter too foreign and unknown. Soldiers at the Front often regarded Saxons and Bavarians as a far more reasonable foe than the automaton Prussians (and from first-hand accounts, it seems that German unification had done little to commend the Prussians to their own – Saxon regiments departing from the front-line trenches would often shout to the British trenches, recommending they give the incoming Prussians 'what for'). Regional loyalties ignored, artists poked fun at the typical German occupations of waiters and musicians and mocked their fondness for sausages. Germans were depicted as square-headed, beady-eyed and bespectacled, with thick moustaches, efficient spiked hair and porcine features. German ingenuity and ability to dream up horrific new ways to kill their enemy was given a comic angle by Heath Robinson, whose 'Frightful War Pictures' depicted increasingly mind-boggling ways to overcome the British. The Kaiser, the ultimate pantomime villain, was a gift to most humorous artists, along with his henchmen, the Kronprinz Wilhelm, Admiral von Tirpitz and Count von Zeppelin. Even the innocent Dachshund did not escape the caricaturist's pen.

'Berlin', Lester Ralph, *The Sketch*, 30 August 1899

Almost 30 years since the Franco-Prussian War and 15 years before World War I, this vision of Berlin as a centre of martial obsession represents a way of life that was looked upon with unease and distaste by the British. All German men were liable to be called upon to do national service for the first two years of adult life and for the subsequent five years were obliged to return to their regiment annually for training. The result was a society with deeply entrenched warlike characteristics, headed by a sovereign who vainly pursued military aggrandisement. Germany's rearmament and naval expansion were, without a doubt, a contributing factor to the simmering tensions that would eventually lead to war in Europe. In 1914, Britain's army stood at only around 247,000. In comparison, Germany's, whose system of peacetime conscription had been accelerated and expanded in an 'arms race' in the years leading up to 1914, was around 864,000.

'Troops passing before the Emperor on the Opera Place', artist unknown, *The Illustrated London News*, 1 July 1871

The Franco-Prussian War of 1870–71 established Germany as the major power of mainland Europe. The annexation of the previously French territory of Alsace-Lorraine by Germany was a source of permanent anguish to France, aggravated by Wilhelm I being crowned Kaiser of the newly unified Germany in the Hall of Mirrors at Versailles. The victory was the pinnacle of an aggressive foreign policy that had seen wars against Denmark and Austria in the 1860s, and an inherent belief in the superiority of German 'Kultur' (culture). The dazzling magnificence of these Prussian troops marching through Paris embodies the elitism of the militaristic Prussians.

'Close Formation', Philip Haynes, *The Bystander*, 26 August 1914
The caption accompanying this picture makes reference to a comment made by the Kaiser to General Sir Ian Hamilton when the Englishman was asked his opinion of the German tactic of 'close formation'. Hamilton suggested, 'Does it not needlessly risk a lot of lives?' to which the Kaiser replied, with a sweep of the hand, 'We can afford to lose them.' Whether the comment was true or not, this picture demonstrates that the humanitarian British frowned upon the German leader's apparent callous disregard for life. In 1914, the German population was 67 million, with an increasing birth rate. Britain's was 46 million and France's 36 million, although no nation could compete with Russia's 164 million. By the end of the war, Germany had lost 1.8 million men out of the 11 million it had mobilised.

'Half-time', George Studdy, *The Bystander*, 25 November 1914

Just two months into the war, this colour cartoon by George Studdy, with a battered and bruised dragon representing the damaged might of Prussian militarism, brings to mind a sporting contest. Entitling the picture 'Half-time' in November 1914 seems hugely optimistic in retrospect, but many still believed the war would only last a matter of months. While the Kaiser, looking miniscule and rather desperate, fans down his beleaguered monster, the Allies sit comfortably at a table, safe in the knowledge that they deserve a moment to enjoy a Christmas pudding. (© George Studdy/ILN Picture Library)

Above: 'Kultur', unattributed artist, *The Bystander*, 14 October 1914
Right: 'Before the War: German soldiers engaging in target practice', Alick P. F. Ritchie, *The Bystander*, 28 October 1914

Germany's conduct during the march through Belgium in the first few weeks of the war bolstered the Allies' stereotypical view of German 'Kultur' as ignorant, barbaric, cruel and uncivilised. The invasion of 'brave, little Belgium' had been tackled with particular brutality by the conscript German troops, who were ordered to respond viciously to any resistance and implement a deliberate policy of 'Schrecklichkeit' (frightfulness). The reports that eventually ended up in the British press were inevitably exaggerated for dramatic and propagandist effect, as was the Bryce report of May 1915, which officially reported on German atrocities and had a huge impact on increasing anti-German sentiment, especially in the United States. However, there was undoubted evidence of hostage-taking, prisoners being shot, human shields being used, and rape being committed, as well as widespread looting. An estimated 20,000 to 30,000 buildings were destroyed, not during fighting but instead from malicious burning. Wholesale destruction of precious medieval buildings, such as the world-famous university library at Louvain, prompted reactions of moral outrage from the international community. *The Bystander*, whose observations were largely intelligent and objective, still published numerous anti-German illustrations, although the message was sophisticated in comparison to the scaremongering and jingoism of some publications.

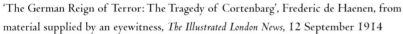

'The German Reign of Terror: The Tragedy of Cortenbarg', Frederic de Haenen, from material supplied by an eyewitness, *The Illustrated London News*, 12 September 1914

Frederic de Haenen was one of the *ILN*'s staff artists, whose job was to translate the sketches of the 'specials' (those who visited the seat of war) or to draw an acceptable, censor-friendly version of events from eyewitness accounts. De Haenen often worked in partnership with Frederic Villiers, the roving artist-correspondent of the *ILN* who spent a great amount of time at the Front. This picture, reporting German reprisals to Belgian resistance in the town of Cortenbarg, shows women, children and the elderly being rounded up, escaping civilians being shot and houses being set alight. Like battlefield actions, scenes such as this were rarely captured candidly on camera and pictures such as these were the only way readers at home could envisage and understand the progress (and reality) of the war.

'She died like a heroine', A. Forestier, *The Illustrated London News*, 30 October 1915

Norfolk-born Edith Louisa Cavell was head of the L'Ecole Infirmiere Dimplonier, a pioneering nursing school on the outskirts of Brussels, which became a Red Cross hospital in 1914, treating the wounded regardless of nationality. Cavell helped some 200 British soldiers escape through the hospital aided by a secret network of Belgian resistance workers, and when the German authorities became suspicious, she was arrested and court-martialled. Her execution by firing squad on 12 October 1915 prompted an international outcry, as well as a media frenzy which included a glut of extreme, allegorical pictures such as this one by Amédée Forestier, notable for the youthful appearance of the fifty-year-old nurse. Yet again, the most valuable propaganda work was done inadvertently by the Germans whose crime was leapt upon by the Allies and used as recruiting propaganda.

'The Abuse of the White Flag: An Incident Showing how our Men were Cut Down by
An Ambushed Envoy', Fortunino Matania, *The Sphere*, 2 January 1915

From the British point of view, German perfidy knew no bounds and extended beyond Belgium and onto

the battlefield. This drawing by Matania, taken from the eyewitness account of Sergeant Megarry, of the
Northamptonshire Regiment, confirms the Teutonic reputation for underhand and unchivalrous tactics.

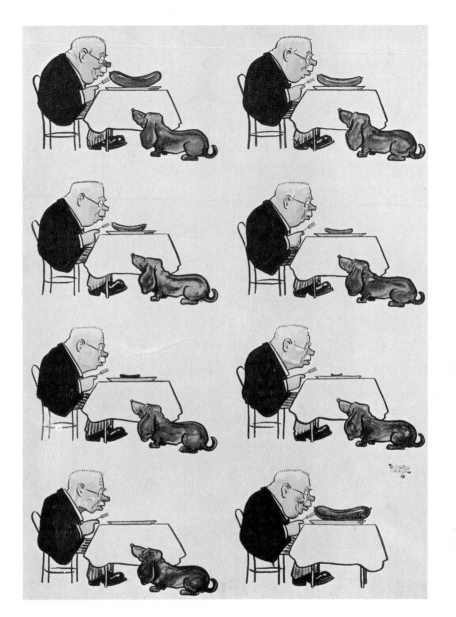

'Beware of the Dog! – A Stern Reminder', Lawson Wood, *The Illustrated Sporting and Dramatic News*, 28 November 1914

The bulldog, sturdy and unwavering, was the ultimate symbol of patriotism and he crops up as a regular during the war years. This one has shown he is no pushover by sinking his teeth into the foot of a passing German soldier in a French village (signifying how British troops had thwarted a swift German invasion in August and September 1914). Lawson Wood gives the soldier epaulettes embroidered with the word, 'Hun', a cocked porkpie hat and a profile not dissimilar to that of his attacker; even his waxed moustache mimics a bulldog's grouchy jaw. (© Estate of Lawson Wood/ILN Picture Library)

'Lost Dog: The Wurst Story of the War', Alfred Leete, *The Bystander*, 14 June 1916

Never has the nickname 'sausage dog' been more appropriate! The Germans suffered from serious food shortages during the war (bread rationing was introduced in Berlin in January 1915), as the decreasing size of this German man's dinner shows. The unwitting Dachshund, a breed popularised in England by Queen Victoria, suffered a temporary fall from grace during and after the war, because of its Germanic origins.

Above: 'Painfully conspicuous', Arthur Watts, *The Bystander*, 4 November 1914
Caption: *'Why Gretchen, what a shame, there's a poor soldier who hasn't been given the Iron Cross'*
Right: 'The Work that Never Ceases', unattributed artist, *The Bystander*, 14 October, 1914
Caption: *The scene at Krupp's works, Essen, where the colossal work of producing iron crosses for distribution by the Kaiser goes on ceaselessly night and day*
During World War I, around 4,000,000 Iron Crosses of the 2nd class order (as well as 145,000 of the higher order) were issued. One of the most famous holders of the Iron Cross 1st class in 1914 was one Adolf Hitler. The huge multitude of awards given out rapidly diminished the Iron Cross's worth and reputation, a fact that the British quickly raised to ridicule. In Arthur Watts's picture, two schoolgirls pity an unembellished soldier (in contrast to the band of swooning schoolgirls admiring a British soldier in Watts's picture on page 143), while the Krupp factory in Essen, working day and night to churn out the tonnes of crosses, is a Stygian hell presided over by a manic demon. The infamous Big Bertha gun, able to fire 16½ inch shells, made reference to the impressive girth of the wife of Gustav von Bohlen, head of the Krupp's steelworks.

'The Force of Habit', Will Owen, *The Sketch*, 8 September 1915

Caption: *The examining officer: 'Whatever induced you to cross to our trenches?'*
Fritz, the waiter: 'I 'ear somepoddy call out "Bill!"' und I rush ober t'inking it vos a gustomer.'

A world away from the brutish, marauding Hun, this rather gormless German POW conjures up an entirely different stereotype. As the caption shows, comic artists took a wicked delight in mimicking the German accent. Before the war, many Germans had worked in London and other towns such as Brighton and Blackpool as barbers, cab drivers and, frequently, waiters. One German soldier, who had worked at the Savoy, recalled how, shortly after the war had started, British soldiers would shout 'Waiter' across their newly dug positions. It was obviously a standing joke.

'Iron-ical!', Alfred Leete, *The Sketch*, 25 November 1914

Caption: *Turkey: 'I wonder – what did William mean when he said: "If you get to the other side, you'll get a Cross?"'*
In comparison to Germany, her Austrian and Turkish allies escaped the cartoonist's sharpest barbs. This hapless Turk, hookah pipe attached to his pack, looks with puzzlement at the Suez Canal which he's been sent to attack by the Kaiser. The picture is a reference to Turkey's long march from Damascus across the Sinai Desert to attack the Suez Canal, the gateway to Egypt. Having crossed the desert without losing a single man, on arrival they found nine British warships and 30,000 British and Indian troops waiting for them, forcing a retreat back into the desert having lost 1,200 men. The expedition had been undertaken with German advice.

Above: 'German Breaches of the Hague Convention: Laughing-Gassing the British Before An Advance in Close Formation', W. Heath Robinson, *The Sketch*, 18 August 1915
Right: 'German Breaches of the Hague Convention: Shepherding Flu Germs into the British Trenches', W. Heath Robinson, *The Sketch*, 30 June 1915

Heath Robinson stands out as one of the truly great illustrators of the Great War. In his autobiography, he writes of how war immediately forced any artistic output to be connected with the 'all-absorbing topic', but Heath Robinson, a man with an astonishingly fruitful imagination, rose to the challenge. During the war, almost all of his pictures were published either by *The Sketch* or *The Bystander* and they played an important role in lifting the spirits of the men in the trenches, hundreds of whom wrote to Robinson suggesting new ideas for his series, 'German Breaches of the Hague Convention'. He admitted that the humour artist's idea of the German soldier 'in the early stages of hostilities was mainly derived from old news pictures of the Franco-Prussian War. It was only later that we abandoned these anachronisms.' Although executed in the most light-hearted way possible, 'Breaches of the Hague Convention' nevertheless depicts the Germans as the side coming up with the most devious devices. Heath Robinson had already displayed his prophetic powers by a pre-war series called 'Am Tag', predicting a German invasion of the British Isles, and he does it again with his flu germ joke; as many as 40 million people worldwide would die from the flu pandemic of 1918. (© Mrs J. C. Robinson by kind permission of the proprietor and Pollinger Limited/ILN Picture Library)

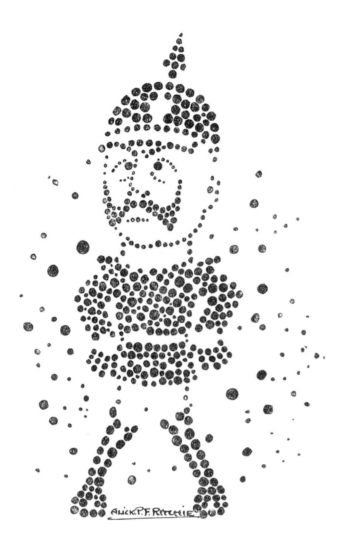

Above: 'Absolutely Dotty', Alick P. F. Ritchie, *The Bystander*, 28 October 1914
Right: 'Wilhelm: "I discard your uniforms and your orders"
John Bull: "The honour is mine"', Alick P. F. Ritchie, *The Bystander*, 2 September 1914

Kaiser Wilhelm II is one of the most psychologically complex characters of World War I. The son and heir of the Crown Prince and Princess of Prussia, his mother, Vicky, had been the eldest child of Queen Victoria and Prince Albert. His birth in 1859 had been difficult and the use of forceps to save mother and child left 'Willie' (as he was known in the family) with a withered arm which he was always at pains to disguise. Vicky had arrived at the Prussian court at the age of 17 filled with enlightened, liberal ideas and the hopes and dreams of her father. But the ruling Emperor, Wilhelm I, was in thrall to the 'blood and iron' Chancellor Bismarck, whose plans for Germany could not have been more different. With her modern English ways despised, the birth of a less-than-perfect heir to the Imperial throne filled her with anxiety and led to a mother–son relationship fraught with tension. To his mother's despair, Willie was taken under the wing of Bismarck. The Chancellor was a brilliant politician who had ensured

Germany's prominence on the European stage with careful diplomatic juggling post-1871, but Willie absorbed the most extreme aspects of Bismarck's policies and became imbued with an elitist and obsessive militarism. As Emperor, Willie was ambitious and neurotically insecure, perhaps 'completely dotty' as Ritchie's picture suggests. He attempted to dominate his immediate family, and the far more laid-back King Edward VII only just managed to tolerate his nephew's bombastic behaviour. Both men shared a love of military uniform, though Willie's was to the point of fetishism, a fact that another of Ritchie's cartoons highlights. On a visit to Cowes in 1889, Willie was keen to inspect British naval equipment, declaring that one day the German fleet would excel that of England. It was unfortunate that, during the jostling power play in the lead up to World War I, such a man was the embodiment of a nation with a deeply entrenched sense of superiority. It is also paradoxical that, although his vainglorious sabre-rattling did much to contribute to tensions on the European stage, he nevertheless concealed a latent streak of Anglophilia. In the summer of 1914, he supported Austrian demands on Serbia, but then did attempt to avoid the inevitable outcome. As the war progressed, power passed into the hands of his more resolute and experienced generals, and, contrary to the popular image of him as a warlord, he became less involved in military strategy as the war continued. As Edward VII astutely observed in 1905, 'It is not by his will that he will unleash a war, but by his weakness.'

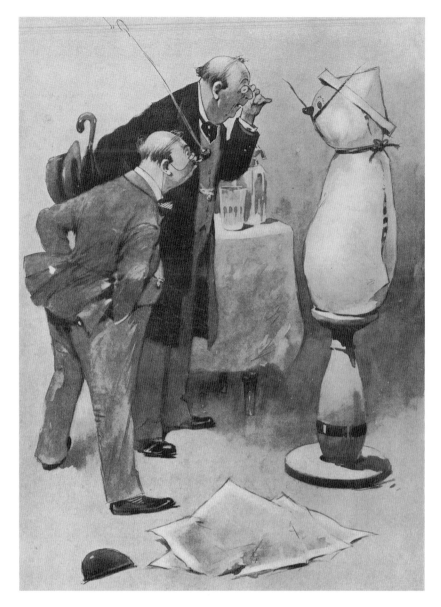

'A Guy – Sir!', George Studdy, *The Sketch*, 4 November 1914

Caption: *The visitor: 'I say, old man, what on earth is this?'*
Little Smithkins: 'That? Oh, that's my Kaiser. Whenever I think of Louvain, or atrocities and things, I go and knock him off his bally pedestal.'

With his unmistakable gravity-defying moustache, this home-made kaiser acts as a punch bag for an irate British citizen, whenever he thinks of the Belgian atrocities. Far from the fighting, and fed inflated stories by the press, many on the home front needed an outlet for their anger, and the German emperor, a man born to be caricatured, became the central focus for anti-German feeling. (© George Studdy/ILN Picture Library)

'As Others See Him: A Birthday Card For the Emperor', Edmund Sullivan, *The Graphic* front cover, 30 January 1915

Edmund Sullivan stands out from other British illustrators as a true original. His dynamic, almost macabre linear drawings were constructed within a sharply defined rectangle and the bristling energy of his looming figures seems imprisoned within its borders. Sullivan's book of anti-German drawings, *The Kaiser's Garland*, published in 1915, echoed the savagery of his European contemporaries, notably that of Louis Raemaekers, and was used widely for propaganda purposes.

'Being Unable to Take Paris', Edwin Morrow, *The Bystander*, 14 October 1914

The Kaiser's eldest son, Crown Prince Wilhelm, was another figure of fun in the British media and was variously depicted as cowardly, wily and corrupt. He was commander of the German Fifth Army and served throughout the war, earning respect in Germany for his victory at Ardennes and his part in the offensives at Verdun and Aisne. However, the British preferred to portray him as a sneak and a thief. This cartoon by Edwin Morrow is based on a claim by the Baroness de Boye, who reported that the Crown Prince had helped himself to a number of valuables and art treasures from her chateau.

'The Fighting Spirit of the British', Fortunino Matania, *The Sphere* front cover, 13 February 1915

This touching scene by Matania stands in stark contrast to the countless anti-German illustrations that were filling magazines but it has still been manipulated in the British soldier's favour, highlighting as it does the innate compassion, and, of course, 'fighting spirit' of the British. The picture is based on a letter sent to *The Manchester Guardian* by a soldier who, '…stopped for a few seconds by the side of a German who was dying. He was in great pain, and when I asked what I could do for him, he said, in a pathetic tone that went to my heart, "Nothing, unless you would be so good as to hold my hand until all is over." I gave him my hand and stayed to the end. It seemed to comfort the poor chap a lot. He was able to speak good English and we had quite a pleasant chat, considering the circumstances. He thought the war would last another year at least, but had no doubt that his own country would be beaten in the end. "Our people didn't make allowance for the fighting spirit of the British", he said.'

From Plug Street to Regent Street

Life in the Trenches

The war may have been a global conflict, but for many it is synonymous with one dominant feature – the trench of the Western Front. The military historian John Ellis wrote, 'For the public, the First World War was the war in the trenches.' After all, the sizeable majority of British soldiers came under fire on the Western Front, and its tangible proximity (the rumbling guns were usually audible in Kent) brought the war almost to Britain's doorstep. Official photographs and flickering newsreels document the rubble and mud of these subterranean lairs. They show grinning troops marching at top speed up the line, hunkering around Tommy cookers or disappearing over the sandbagged parapet into a misty oblivion. These images are etched on our psyche and, as if to mark the significance of trench warfare, the original troughs and furrows, though filled in and overgrown, still form an undulating pattern across the French landscape. They serve as an indelible reminder of a conflict that reduced serene rural fields to a shell-pocked wasteland.

During the course of the war, five million soldiers from both sides experienced life in the trenches. With such impressive statistics, it is hardly surprising that the trials and tribulations of trench life created a prevailing theme for artists.

The trench was where men lived and died. It was where they ate their bully beef, smoked their 'gaspers' and groaned on discovering that the new batch of standard issue jam was plum and apple yet again. It was where men waged war not just on the enemy, but on the rats, lice and trench foot, as well as on the

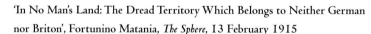

'In No Man's Land: The Dread Territory Which Belongs to Neither German nor Briton', Fortunino Matania, *The Sphere*, 13 February 1915
Royal Engineers, working in the dark of No Man's Land to construct barbed wire barriers in front of British trenches, are exposed by German magnesium flares, giving this illustration a Caravaggioesque quality. Such work was extremely risky, or 'nervy', as one Royal Engineer described it to *The Times*. He went on to say, '…it is done in the open and out of the kindly cover afforded by a trench…fortunate indeed is the working party if the enemy does not hear the sound of the pickets being driven into the ground and open fire…'. Flares lasted for 15 seconds, an eternity for men who had to throw themselves flat to the ground and lie inert until darkness returned. Bruce Bairnsfather depicted a similar situation in a cartoon accompanied by a quote from Wolfram's aria in *Tannhauser*.
'Oh star of eve, whose tender beam
Falls on my spirit's troubled dream.'

endless mud and flooding. Trench life was uncomfortable, repetitive and often dull, yet it was a monotony punctuated by episodes of quite indescribable horror. One 'eyewitness', describing trench life in *The Graphic* in January 1915, called it 'a strange, cramped existence, with death always near, either by means of some missile from above or some mine explosion from beneath; a life which has one dull, monotonous background of mud and water.' The British took pride in tolerating the chronic conditions and tedium with fortitude, stoicism and a humour that resonated in many illustrations. Nobody summed this up better than Bruce Bairnsfather, whose own experience of the trenches bolstered his talent for affectionately caricaturing the recognisable 'types' in the British army.

Trenches may have characterised World War I, but contrary to popular assumption, the concept was not new to the British army. *Field Service Regulations*, published in 1909, and *Infantry Training* of 1914 both emphasised the importance of the trench, and instructed where to locate and how to build them. This advice was not always easy to follow. The Western Front stretched roughly 740km from the North Sea to the Swiss border, and terrain and geology dictated the style and structure of a trench system: the chalk of Artois was notoriously difficult to excavate, but tenacious diggers would be rewarded with sturdy walls, unlike the soft earth of the Ypres salient, which caused countless difficulties.

Trench warfare may not have been a new idea, but it had never been implemented on such a scale and for such a long period. A huge infrastructure began to build up behind the front-line trench. Communication trenches would run adjacent, their purpose to feed men, munitions and supplies through to the front, while support trenches offered backup and a place to retreat to if necessary. Dug-outs, some quite elaborately furnished, appeared sporadically along each trench, and such were the maze-like qualities of most trench systems that many routes were fondly named after familiar streets from home, or jokingly anglicised French names.

The routine of trench life would usually require battalions to serve in the fire (front) trench for up to seven days, before service in the support trenches for a week and then a week off before beginning the cycle once more. While in the front line, sleeping arrangements for most soldiers were rudimentary, rarely more than a 'funk hole' scraped in the side of the trench wall.

Squelching boots and a dearth of home comforts meant that small, simple pleasures were savoured. Army issue cigarettes kept the British army going through four years of war, and presents from family, especially at Christmas, were an eagerly anticipated lifeline to home. Magazine advertisements quickly espoused the essential nature of their products for men at the Front, such as Zam-buk ointment ('Our Soldiers at the Front Urgently Need More Zam-buk') or Zambrene weatherproofs ('absolutely defies the elements as no other raincoat will do'), Gong Soups ('Gong Soups are "Top Hole"') and even Decca portable gramophones ('Mirth-maker in Chief to the Army and Navy').

Magazines sent to the Front were greatly enjoyed, passed around and eventually cut up to decorate the walls of dug-outs. In particular, *The Sketch* and *The Bystander* were popular, combining gossip and humour with a whiff of glamour to brighten a Tommy's day. In the early months of the war, *The Tatler* boasted in its advertising that it was going to eschew war news for more pleasant subjects. But the war pervaded everything and *The Tatler* could not distance itself for long. It was through the most popular magazines that spirits were lifted, and soldiers were touchingly reminded that those at home had not forgotten them. *The Bystander* in particular encouraged soldier-artists, amateur or otherwise, to send in their work for publication. Any artist who had a perceptive knack for recreating Tommy's experiences and depicting his humour would rarely be short of commissions. The trick was to find comedy in even the bleakest moments, without belittling those involved, a skill Bairnsfather pulled off deftly, receiving floods of letters from soldier fans, who recognised either themselves or their comrades in his creations.

The cycle of duty included coming out of line; a welcome relief. Soldiers might enjoy the charms of the local *estaminet* or simply the comfort of a makeshift bed in the attic of their billets. But the pleasure of time off would always be blighted by the knowledge that the next 'big push' might be just days away. Death could come at any time to men serving in the trenches — from sniper bullets, shell fire, mortar explosions or gas — but going 'over the top' remained a ghastly inevitability. Hundreds of thousands of soldiers did just that, and were never to return. There is a deep poignancy in remembering that, for them, the trench was their final home.

'The Army takes over a Chateau – And the Staff moves in!', R. O. E. Prancer, *The Bystander*, 8 May 1918
A picture that plays to popularly accepted stereotypes shows hundreds of soldiers, busy preparing a French chateau as an HQ, only for a solitary, albeit substantial, general (and his

dog) to move in. The term 'chateau generalship' has sprung out of the lexicon of World War I, suggesting that those in command were out of touch with what was happening on the front line, often several miles away. In truth, brigades and divisions needed headquarters; big houses, and often chateaux, were a practical choice. Some regimental soldiers had an aversion to staff officers, nicknamed 'Red Tabs' or 'Brass Hats'. One officer in the Royal Irish Rifles remarked that the red tabs on staff uniform were 'the insignia of hopeless inefficiency'.

'Tommy (trench-digging): I'm about fed up with this. Won't it be grand when it's all over and we can go back to work', Stan Terry, *The Tatler*, 28 February 1917
There would have been no trenches without men to dig them, and doing so was back-breaking work. In some battalions, officers worked alongside their men; in others the practice was actively discouraged. The construction of trenches, dug-outs and even 'funk holes' for sleeping was better-suited to those who were used to physical work. The 230,000 miners who enlisted during the war could put their skills to good use, not just in digging trenches but in the work of the Royal Engineers, tunnelling and laying mines. By 1915, funk holes were discouraged as they tended to weaken trench walls and dug-outs became prevalent. These varied in size and sophistication, but few matched the German versions, some of which were as deep as 60 feet and entirely impervious to shell explosions. One English officer, writing in *The Graphic* in December 1914, obviously had great pride in the British trenches: 'I wish you could walk around our trenches and see all the loopholes, front entanglements, perfect traverses – thus to minimise enfilading fire; the shelters are beneath recesses in which men lie, and then by guarded passage descend to the main street. You should see our dug-outs, some roofed, as our mess is, with boards and doors and earth on these to make our quarters rainproof. The men too have made themselves a roof; to see them cook their meals in any kind of tin would surprise you.'

Above: 'Sunshine and Dust Near Neuville St.Vaast – A Scene on the British Lines of Communication', Captain Edward Handley-Read, *The Sphere*, 31 August 1918
Opposite: 'No Man's Land – A Study on the British Western Front', Captain Edward Handley-Read, *The Sphere*, 21 September 1918

Captain Edward Handley-Read exhibited his war landscapes at The Alpine Club Gallery in Conduit Street in the West End of London in June and July of 1918, his third such exhibition at the gallery since 1916. It attracted the attention of the Queen and Princess Mary who are recorded as visiting it on 19 June. Handley-Read, though 45 years old at the outbreak of war, was a quartermaster sergeant instructor with the Machine Gun Corps (but had previously been in the Artists' Rifles), moving on to second lieutenant and then captain by the time of this exhibition. The pictures present two very different views of the Western Front: the stark, alien mire of No Man's Land, which would have met the gaze of any sentry peering across to the enemy trenches, against the road leading up to the British line, brightly lit by sunshine. The landscape is still bleak, but it is easy to forget that in between the episodes of rain and mud, there could be devilishly hot weather too – another problem for British soldiers who were only issued with the scratchy wool khaki more suited to chilly temperatures. Some improvised by cutting their trousers into shorts.

'In the Famous "Plug Street" Wood – A Relief Party Marching Back to the Trenches through "Regent Street"',
Fortunino Matania, *The Sphere*, 29 May 1915

Fortunino Matania visited the Front on several occasions, and this illustration of a relief party going back 'up the line' was drawn from first-hand experience. 'Plug Street' was the Anglicised nickname for Ploegstreet Wood, south of the Ypres salient. It was a notoriously quiet spot, but many died from isolated shelling or sniping activity, evidenced by the scarred trees lining the soldiers' route. Matania points out in his accompanying description that the men are in no danger, as a 'long line of sand bags, a little higher than a man, provided sufficient defence'. The men in the picture carry the belongings they will need for this stint in the front line. According to a German account in the *Berliner Zeitung am Mittag*, German soldiers capturing a British trench were delighted to find 'a mass of excellent preserves, corned beef and ham, and many also secured one of the shaving outfits which nearly every English soldier carries'.

'The Long and the Short of It', Bruce Bairnsfather, *The Bystander*, 30 August 1916

Caption: *Up last draft: 'I suppose you 'as to be careful 'ow you looks over the parapet about 'ere'*
Out since Mons: 'You needn't worry me lad, the rats are going to be your only trouble'

Bruce Bairnsfather loved to contrast the world-weary, hardened old hand who had been 'Out since Mons' with the naïve raw recruit. But his joke does stress two perennial problems for trench inhabitants – the danger from snipers (for those who either dared to look over the sandbags, or were unfortunate enough to be tall), and the constant battle with the hoards of impudent rats, encouraged by unburied bodies and discarded food.

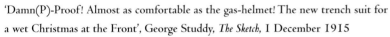

'Damn(P)-Proof! Almost as comfortable as the gas-helmet! The new trench suit for a wet Christmas at the Front', George Studdy, *The Sketch*, 1 December 1915

The trenches could be far more than damp. They could be completely waterlogged. Sometimes, soldiers found themselves waist-deep in water, usually due to atrocious weather. The soft ground of Belgium resulted in trenches collapsing in places during wet periods, and the task of draining and repairs, under the Royal Engineers, might take hundreds of men and seem endless. Studdy's all-in-one waterproof suit may turn his soldiers into rather forlorn-looking primeval mutants, but would probably have been preferable to the khaki uniform and, worse, to goatskin coats, which only made the wearer more uncomfortable and less agile once wet. (© George Studdy/ILN Picture Library)

'The British Line – No.1 "Wipers"', 'Snaffles', *The Illustrated Sporting and Dramatic News*, 29 May 1915

This picture by 'Snaffles' aka Charles Johnson Payne (1883–1967) was published shortly after the Second Battle of Ypres in May 1915, in which Germans used gas for the first time. Despite large losses on both sides, the Germans failed to gain ground from the British and this soldier, encumbered by his spade and a wounded hand, personifies the gritty determination displayed by the various British (and Canadian) battalions involved. Snaffles built his reputation as a sporting artist, focusing especially on hunting subjects, and his military pictures echo this imagery – from the defeated Germans lying at his feet, to his trophy, a Pickelhaube helmet, atop his bayonet. 'Wipers' was a British colloquialism, replacing the difficult pronunciation of Ypres.

'"High" Explosive', E. H. Shepard, *The Sketch*, 13 October 1915

Caption: *Giving the Germans the Bird: A substitute for the shell lachrymatory and the bomb malodorous — a pheasant from home*

Parcels from home were eagerly awaited, especially food parcels, which provided a welcome diversion from the monotony of army rations. Although parcels could arrive at the Front within as little as four days, others might take weeks as in the case of this pheasant, which is instead fired from a gun as a worthy alternative to shell fire. Bert Thomas used the same joke a month later in *The Bystander*, but instead the soldier used his Aunt Matilda's Xmas pudding! E. H. Shepard is best known for his charming illustrations for A. A. Milne's *Winnie the Pooh* and Kenneth Grahame's *The Wind in the Willows*, but his most prolific work was for *Punch*. He also produced a number of pictures for *The Sketch* during World War I, despite a commission in the Royal Artillery. He was in the battles of the Somme, Arras and Ypres and ended the war serving as Major Shepard MC in Italy.

'The Eternal Question "When the 'ell is it going to be strawberry?" (Plum and apple is the only jam known throughout the whole Expeditionary Force)', Bruce Bairnsfather, *The Bystander* front cover, 15 September 1915

The ubiquitous standard issue plum and apple jam was much derided, as Bairnsfather's Old Bill attests in this cover picture from *The Bystander*. Plum and apple joined bully beef (tinned corned beef) and hard biscuits as standard rations, supplemented by tinned meat and vegetables of varying quality known as Maconochie, after Maconochie Brothers of London, the main manufacturer of the stew.

'Christmas at the Front – Unpacking the Parcels from Home', Fortunino Matania,
The Sphere, 5 January 1918

The editorial beneath this picture reports that 'The arrival of the post is always an event
which is eagerly awaited by the men at the Front, particularly at Christmas time'. This hamper
includes a plum pudding, giving a festive air to the proceedings. Parcels were usually distributed
once men were out of the line, and their contents were pooled, ensuring everyone was able to
savour the occasional luxury.

'Weinachtszeit', Christopher Clark, *The Sphere*, 9 January 1915

While in the line at Armentières in December 1914, *Bystander* artist Bruce Bairnsfather
experienced one of the most legendary episodes in the whole war – the Christmas truce.
Along many sectors of the Front, on Christmas Eve and Christmas Day, British and German
soldiers warily began to emerge from their opposing trenches and met in No Man's Land to
exchange photographs, cigarettes and mementoes. Bairnsfather described how 'one of the
Boches ran back to his trench and presently reappeared with a large camera. I posed in a mixed
group for several photographs, and have ever since wished I had fixed up some arrangement
for getting a copy.' This picture recalls a similar incident.

Above: 'The Surreys Play the Game: Kicking Footballs Towards the German Trenches under a Hail of Shells',
R. Caton Woodville, *The Illustrated London News*, 29 July 1916
Right: 'Our Happy Tommies', John E. Sutcliffe, *The Illustrated Sporting and Dramatic News*, 17 October 1914

A typically upbeat choice of subject for *The Illustrated Sporting and Dramatic News*, Sutcliffe's illustration records a football match played by troops in a French village 'place' somewhere along the British second line during the battle of the Aisne. The caption reminds the reader that 'many footballs have been sent to France for use in the ranks'. The picture, as well as the title, conveys a positive image of trench life and would have given comfort to those at home to know that their men occasionally had fun. But football also embodied the British spirit of fair play, a symbolism that also found credence on the battlefield. On the first day of the Somme, Captain W. B. Nevill, attached to the 8th East Surreys, provided four footballs for his platoons and urged them to keep up a dribbling competition on their way to the German trenches. Nevill was shot down just before the German wire, but his enterprising idea posthumously reaped rewards as his battalion helped take the Montauban Ridge and won several military awards for their bravery. R. Caton Woodville was the master of painting the valiant charge. This impression of the East Surreys, though perhaps not his most accomplished, and despite modifying reality (the ground is completely free of wire), is nevertheless a rousing tribute to both the regiment's heroism and its sporting prowess.

'Libellous? – With a Sporting Battalion at the Front: Highly Imaginative Drawings',
Harry Low, *The Sketch*, 11 August 1915

The over-enthusiasm of Harry Low's sporting battalion certainly raises a smile. There were many such battalions, including the 1st Football Battalion (aka 17/Middlesex) and the Sportsmen's Battalion (23/Royal Fusiliers), which included two England cricketers as well as the country's lightweight boxing champion. Despite the mocking tone of this cartoon, the British greatly admired sporting ability and substantial coverage was often given to the many talented sportsmen who lost their lives, such as Anthony Wilding, the New Zealand-born tennis champion who was killed by a shell explosion at Neuve Chapelle in May 1915.

'Concerned!', Wilmot Lunt, *The Tatler*, 3 February 1915

Caption: *Disappointed Tommy to Officer (after waiting several hours for an expected assault by the enemy which has not come off): 'I do hope as 'ow nothin' serious 'as 'appened to the poor devils, sir'*

In some areas of the Western Front, there was a 'live and let live' attitude towards the enemy and many British soldiers retained a grudging respect for their German counterparts. Wiring parties or stretcher-bearers would often work parallel to each other in No Man's Land at night, and there was occasional banter thrown from trench to opposite trench. For those who had first-hand experience of German humanity, it often took the death of comrades to stir them into retaliation.

'C'est la Guerre, mais ce n'est pas magnifique – The interior of a signal "office" somewhere in France. – Time: 2am', Trooper J. G. Cowell, Warwickshire Yeomanry, *The Bystander* front cover, 16 February 1916

The wretched look on this signaller's face speaks volumes. Many who joined Kitchener's New Army in the opening weeks of the war did so expecting adventure and excitement. Many were petrified that it would all be over before they could get there. The gruelling, mud-soaked, uncomfortable, bloody reality of trench warfare, as well as the endless tedium, was a shocking disappointment to many. The quote is a twist on that belonging to a French general, Pierre Bosquet, commenting on the reckless bravery of the charge of the Light Brigade in 1854.

'Rejected by the Inventions Board VIII – The Harley-Scope Mine-Detector', W. Heath Robinson, *The Sketch*, 19 January 1916

Mining was an integral part of each side's strategy and the Royal Engineers' tunnelling companies were raised specifically for the business of laying mines. Often working blindly and against time, a mine laid by 178 Tunnelling Company blew the top off Hill 60 on the Ypres Salient on 17 April 1915, just two days before the Germans had planned to do the same. Bigger and more destructive mines were to wreak further damage as the war progressed – at Hooge Ridge on the Menin Road and at La Boiselle on the Somme, which blew a crater 70 feet deep and could be heard in London. Mining could be a lonely and dangerous job, not to mention a strategic race against the German opposite numbers. Sappers working in shafts would often use stethoscopes to listen to the enemy working close by. (© Mrs J. C. Robinson by kind permission of the proprietor and Pollinger Limited/ILN Picture Library)

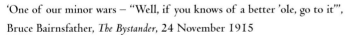

'One of our minor wars – "Well, if you knows of a better 'ole, go to it"',
Bruce Bairnsfather, *The Bystander*, 24 November 1915

A handful of images truly sum up the Great War. Singer Sergant's 'Gassed' and Alfred Leete's recruiting poster are iconic, while Matania's 'Goodbye Old Man' on page 169 of this book appealed to the sentimental British public. Bairnsfather's 'better 'ole' is his best-loved cartoon and stands alongside these images as a military version of that most common of human conditions: discontent. Bairnsfather's biographers, Tonie and Valmai Holt, describe the picture as 'the greener grass proverb in khaki' and the British public, always ready to laugh at themselves, hoovered up the Christmas issue of *The Bystander* in which it appeared.

'Coiffure in the Trenches – "Keep yer 'ead still, or I'll 'ave yer blinkin' ear off"',
Bruce Bairnsfather, *The Bystander*, 10 November 1915

There is an unconscious irony to this barber's comment as shells whiz by dangerously overhead, but Bairnsfather liked to show his battle-weary Tommies coping with the war by concentrating on the minutiae of everyday trench life. The artist's skill in conveying the grumpy, dogged determination of the ordinary British soldier sealed his popularity, and although he was never to achieve the same success after the war, his style and his humour – representing the irrepressible British ability to get on with life, even when all around is chaos – struck a chord of perfect pitch with the public in 1915.

'The Motor Cyclist and the Magic Shell: A Military Fantasy', H. M. Bateman,
The Tatler, 28 November 1917

H. M. Bateman's animated, slightly manic style is perfectly suited to this sequential cartoon showing a motorcyclist being relentlessly pursued by a shell. The arbitrary and indiscriminate nature of shell fire, whether shrapnel or high explosive, was one of the hardest aspects of warfare to bear, and there was little infantry soldiers could do except try to find shelter. The resultant wounds could be horrifying, and yet, while a shell burst might dismember one man, another man close by might escape unharmed. Bateman's nightmarish narrative suggests that some soldiers must have felt that certain shells had their name written on them. (© H. M. Bateman Designs Limited/ILN Picture Library)

'"Somewhere in France" – A Concert Behind the Lines', Fortunino Matania, *The Sphere*, 29 November 1915

Music halls enjoyed a strong following at home and so it was no surprise that concert parties were a popular form of entertainment for men behind the lines. Most shows took the form of a revue, and were a mix of songs and sketches taken from the music halls but adapted to reflect the war's circumstances. Divisional entertainment companies, such as The Whizzbangs, The Verey Lights and The Duds, were made up of professional and amateur actors, many of whom dressed convincingly in drag. Matania visited the Front several times, but a photographic memory meant that notes and rough sketches were usually enough for him to recreate a complete painting back in his studio. Pinpoint accuracy, not just in uniforms but also in surrounding objects, is the hallmark of his work.

'How The Gas Devil Comes – "The Thick Green Mist Came Rolling Towards the Parapet"', F. Matania,
The Sphere, 29 May 1915
On 22 April 1915 at Ypres, the Germans used poisonous chlorine gas for the first time. Despite warnings from captured Germans, the British and French were totally unprepared, with no protection, and began to suffer the effects within minutes. Most had to retreat in disarray, many stayed at their posts – hundreds died. The British press was outraged at this new, insidious raising of the game by the Germans. Sir John French reported of the use: 'The quantity used produced long and deliberate preparation for the employment of devices contrary to the terms of the Hague Convention, to which the enemy subscribed.'

'As it is for most of us', Bruce Bairnsfather, *The Bystander*, 1 March 1916
World War I was a slog, described by many as '90% routine and 10% terror'. Although soldiers lived with death every day, for the most part, major battles were few and far between, and sometimes it was the dread and anticipation of what was to come that was most psychologically damaging, especially for inexperienced new recruits. When an offensive did come, nobody could predict the ferocity or the outcome. Despite commanders' hopes that attacks might take place in an orderly formation, most were a chaotic scrum of noise, smoke, screams and shell fire, as summed up by Bairnsfather's loose, vigorous penmanship.

'The Language of Diplomacy', Will Owen, *The Sketch,* **3 March 1915**

Caption: *Tommy (writing home from a prison camp): 'Dear Maria, everythink 'ere is luvvly: cumfurtable quarters; fine clothes; a 'ome from 'ome. Bill, who was of a differing opinion, was shot yesterday.'*

Surrendering to the enemy could be a lottery, but for some, it was a way to survive the war; however the treatment of prisoners-of-war could vary dramatically on both sides. The British generally treated their German prisoners well, although German treatment of prisoners-of-war could vary dramatically, a fact this Tommy has carefully observed. Will Owen was an artist of the poster school and is best known for his collaboration with the writer W. W. Jacobs, as well as the 'Ah Bisto!' poster.

'Rejected by the Inventions Board: VII – The Gallipoli Shell-Diverter for Returning the Enemy's Fire', by W. Heath Robinson, *The Sketch,* **12 January 1916**

There were other theatres of war besides the Western Front, and after the disastrous landings at Gallipoli off the Dardanelles strait, the soldiers were forced to dig trenches there too. Blistering heat in the summer led to disease, and dysentery killed more men than did bullets. Heath Robinson remembered the soldiers who fought at Gallipoli in his 'Rejected by the Inventions Board' series, although this time his contraptions are scattering Turkish soldiers wearing fez hats, rather than Germans in their Pickelhaube helmets. (© Mrs J. C. Robinson by kind permission of the proprietor and Pollinger Limited/ILN Picture Library)

'The Dream', Mabel Ince, *The Bystander* 7 July 1915

A typical English country garden, timbered house and a saintly sweetheart inhabit the dreams of this slumbering soldier. Mabel Ince's style is prettily decorative, in the tradition of Charles Robinson. Her talents extended beyond illustration, and she was the author of romantic novels whose titles imitate the dreamy romance of her picture – *The Wisdom of Waiting* and *Commonplace and Clementine*, published in 1912 and 1913 respectively.

'The Harvest', J. F. Woolrich, *The Tatler*, 2 September 1914

Caption: *'And with mine own hand labour'd it to grow,*
And this was all the harvest that I reap'd'

The moralising quote, from the *Rubaiyat* of Omar Kyyam, offers no sympathy to this dead German, lying symbolically in a field of wheat. The fate of the bodies of fallen soldiers was dependent on many factors: the stage of battle, the weather, the generosity of the enemy in allowing stretcher-bearers to bring back their dead. Where possible, soldiers tried to bury their fallen comrades with solemnity but in many cases bodies lay where they fell, until they were eventually claimed by the earth. Of the British Empire's dead, the bodies of a staggering 500,000 soldiers were never found.

'The Last Message…If you Get Through…Tell my Mother…', Fortunino Matania,
The Sphere, **26 November 1917**

Death came in many ways to men in World War I: from a sniper's bullet or a vaporising shell blast; from hand-to-hand fighting or prosaically from fumes inhaled from braziers intended only to keep men warm in the winter months. But many hoped and imagined that, if death were to come, it would be on the battlefield as part of an offensive. Testimonies to the final words of some dying soldiers are heart-wrenching – some died quietly and were lucid enough to ask comrades to pass on a message to their families. Others were so badly wounded, they begged to be shot. The best a mortally wounded man could hope for was that he should not die alone.

Above: 'Our Soldiers: How They Are Made – And Mended', H. L. Oakley, *The Bystander*, 21 June 1916

Opposite: 'Staff, Subs, Sentries & Surprises Silhouetted', by H. L. Oakley, *The Bystander*, 24 May 1916

H. L. Oakley was an immensely talented silhouettist who cut portraits of the Prince of Wales, Lloyd George, G. K. Chesterton, Edward Elgar, Donald Bradman, Queen Elizabeth, the Queen Mother (when Duchess of York) and fellow artists Heath Robinson, H. M. Bateman and John Hassall among others. While training in England, he designed two well-known recruiting posters that were accepted by the Parliamentary Recruiting Committee: 'Think!' for the army and 'Remember!' for the navy, designs which were adapted for Commonwealth recruitment campaigns. He contributed to *The Graphic* and *London Opinion* during the war, while serving as a second lieutenant in the 8th Yorkshire Regiment (the Green Howards), but the bulk of his output was for *The Bystander*, with a charming series of silhouettes illustrating life in the trenches. In 1916, Oakley was seriously wounded

Staff, Subs, Sentries, & Surprises Silhouetted

BY AN OFFICER AT THE FRONT

AN OFFICER'S DUG-OUT

A YOUNG SUB

AN ARCADIAN TOUCH

RATIONS

CLEANING RIFLES

A HEATED ARGUMENT

THE STAFF

SENTRIES

A PATROL

OH! I SAY!

THE SILHOUETTIST HIMSELF

DIXIE-LAND (" DIXIE" IS THE NAME GIVEN TO TOMMY'S COOKING POT)

and sent back to hospital in England. The end silhouette on the left could easily be cut from experience. On recovery, he returned to France and was appointed ADC to the Commanding Officer of the 32nd Division, Major General T. S. Lambert. The inherent skill required to produce such art is impressive. When writing of Oakley's work, *The Bystander* commented that his silhouettes, 'cut directly with scissors from paper [have] a freshness and directness of effect which the artist who uses pen or brush cannot obtain'. Oakley earned the MBE, Military Division, in 1919.

Business as Usual

The Home Front

On 16 December 1914, the German High Seas Fleet fired 1,500 shells at Scarborough, West Hartlepool and Whitby on Britain's east coast, resulting in 127 civilian deaths. Total war had arrived, and nobody, not even the civilian population, was safe. World War I affected non-combatants in more ways than any previous conflict. Traditional gender roles were distorted, food and other commodities became increasingly scarce and Britain, for the first time in many centuries, was threatened with regular enemy attacks and even, perhaps, invasion.

The coastal attacks were joined by aerial assaults, with Great Yarmouth and Lowestoft becoming the first victims of the Zeppelin on 3 November 1914. Although lumbering and inefficient as a weapon of war, the Zeppelin was still an ominous threat. Despite their destructive potential, the public was fascinated by these silent sky vessels and the Zeppelin often took front page in illustrated magazines. Two years later, an air raid – in the modern sense – using Gotha G.IV bombers targeted the East Anglian towns once more and a little while later, London. The East End suffered on 13 June 1917 when a daylight raid killed 158 people in Poplar, including, tragically, 18 school children.

There were other less hazardous, but sometimes wearisome, aspects of the civilian's war, some of which have left a legacy that continues today. Daylight saving was introduced in May 1916, designed to save energy and to enable daily industrial production to go on for longer. There was to be no chiming of public clocks between sunset and sunrise, nor whistling for taxi cabs. Most dramatically, public houses closed two and a half hours earlier, at 10pm. Lloyd George famously declared, 'We are fighting Germans, Austrians and Drink, and so far as I can see the greatness of these deadly foes is Drink.'

'The Magic Interlude', Claude Shepperson, *The Tatler*, 10 July 1918
Much as the public wanted pictures that empathised with the hardship of war, there was always room for a little romantic escapism. Claude Shepperson, an artist who was well respected by his contemporaries, painted soft-focus, elegant tableaux recalling lazy summer afternoons or glittering society parties. His figures were always graceful, as are these children, who are momentarily interrupted from a game of tennis by a friendly aeroplane high in the sky. Shepperson died in 1921 at the age of 54. His charming painting style was matched by a charm of manner that earned him the nickname 'the aristocrat who sketched' and his loss was greatly mourned in the artistic community.

By the end of the war, Lloyd George had defeated his prime foe and consumption of alcohol had dropped by half.

Before the war, Britain had imported 60 per cent of her food. With German U-boats targeting British merchant ships and a particularly bad American wheat harvest in 1916, the time had arrived for self-sufficiency, a huge challenge to farmers who found themselves in the unenviable position of having to produce more food with far fewer farmhands and horses. If Britain were to survive by producing her own food, then she must also practise abstemiousness. This was a gradual process. Initially, Lord Devonport, the Food Controller, appealed for voluntary rationing with little success. One poster encouraged the population to 'Save the Wheat, Protect the Fleet – Eat less Bread'. Increasing food shortages eventually led to compulsory rationing, which was imposed nationwide in April 1918. *The Illustrated London News* took up the frugality campaign with enthusiasm. Filomena, its lady columnist, chose to write about the nutritious benefits of wholemeal bread one week: 'We must *all* realise the extreme and immediate necessity of food economy.' In another column, she admonished the Food Controller's office for recommending people eat boiled rhubarb leaves: 'Many people have been made ill by following this advice. Don't do it!' The *ILN* also ran a piece recommending sorrel leaves, dandelion leaves and nettles, as considerably safer alternative greens. Meanwhile, food manufacturers were getting in on the economising act. Goodall, Backhouse & Co. of Leeds recommended their Yorkshire Relish to perk up a lentil roast (recipe included) or their egg powder in cinnamon buns.

Inflation affected clothing as well as food, forcing the fashionable readers of *The Sketch* and *The Tatler* to dream up enterprising ways to remain stylish, or, for the wealthier, to disguise the obvious newness of their clothes – a recurring theme among the humorous artists – and speaks of the magazine's continuing interest in the latest fashions from Paris.

As a whole, the British public rose to the challenge of war. There had been a strong tradition of volunteering in Britain and charitable organisations of all kinds sprang up alongside more established charities like the Red Cross. The great ladies of Edwardian England, spearheaded by Queen Mary herself, went into fundraising overdrive, organising flag days, bazaars or knitting 'comforts' for troops. The Victoria League, which focused on providing hospitality for Commonwealth servicemen, and Queen Mary's Needlework Guild, which utilised the traditional skills of women by sewing or knitting garments of variable quality for the men at the Front, were just two of the support groups active at the time. Men who were too old or unfit to enlist could join volunteer reserves, and thousands of women joined proactive, often military-minded organisations, such as the WVR (Women's Volunteer Reserve) or the WAAC (Women's Army Auxiliary Corps), all eager to do their bit.

Life wasn't all work and no play. Theatres and music halls boomed during the war years, propelled by the increased wealth of the working classes and partly to fill a need for entertaining distraction in what was an otherwise dismal four years. There were around 3,000 cinemas across Britain in 1914, a number that continued to grow despite the war, where audiences were fed a diet of mainly American silent films, starring Charlie Chaplin and Mary Pickford. In theatreland, the huge success of *Chu Chin Chow* and *The Bing Boys are Here* revealed the public's taste for lighter forms of entertainment. Bruce Bairnsfather's Old Bill made it to the stage, first as a sketch in a series of revues, but then as a play in itself, *The Better 'Ole*, which debuted at the Oxford Theatre starring Arthur Bourchier and was later adapted into a 1927 Warner Brothers film.

And of course, the magazines themselves were part of the fabric of everyday life on the home front. They had the dual purpose of informing and entertaining, and they achieved both with admirable success despite the setbacks of censorship and paper shortages. In many ways, the magazines in the *ILN* archive propagated their success by feeding the public what they wanted. By doing so, they are an unparalleled record, a barometer if you like, of the daily lives, concerns and opinions of those on the home front.

'This Fortress, Built by Nature for Herself – Guarding the White Cliffs of Old Albion', Philip Dadd, *The Sphere*, 7 December 1914

If this picture were set to music, it would surely be to something patriotically rousing – perhaps Elgar or Cecil Spring-Rice's 'I Vow to Thee My Country' (admittedly not written until 1918). The editorial describes the White Cliffs of Dover as 'the most spectacular of all the sentries guarding this island realm' of 'Old Albion'. This mythical, almost Arthurian description bestows on proud and impenetrable Britain a sacred status that would have appealed greatly to a nationalistic readership. The White Cliffs, of course, continued to be a national, natural monument, the definition of Britishness in World War II. The picture was painted by Philip Dadd, a *Sphere* 'special artist', and a nephew of Kate Greenaway. He joined the Queen's Westminster Rifles in December 1915, despite doubts about his ability to be a soldier, but, according to his *Sphere* obituary, 'thoroughly enjoyed the camp life and went out to the war full of courage and hope'. Dadd was always able to see the beauty in his surroundings, and wrote letters home, in which he described the trenches as 'a mass of poppies and stuff and glorious to behold'. In another: 'The part we are resting in must have been a lovely spot before the war. One discovers fresh beauties every day. Yesterday evening and this afternoon I lay on top of a hill amongst masses of clover and vetch and looked over miles of country, one way all smiling under calm skies, all mapped out in cultivation of various kinds, the other scarred by trenches, blasted by shot and shell, and echoing to explosions etc.' Philip Dadd was killed in France on 2 August 1916. He is buried in the Maroeuil British cemetery, north of Arras.

'Terrible Revelation of a British Frivolity During a Raid on the East Coast', W. Heath Robinson, *The Illustrated Sporting and Dramatic News*, 23 January 1916

Despite the damage and loss of life inflicted on the east coast, artists managed to find a humorous angle. Here, a vertiginous dwelling, nudged by the tail of a clumsy Zeppelin, opens up to reveal a secret love tryst. Heath Robinson himself was a civilian during the war, and though living in the comparative safety of Pinner in Middlesex, he spoke for all when he wrote 'The Zeppelin menace was beginning to haunt us' but concludes, 'such was the humorous spirit in which we tried to regard the very serious position we were all in at that time', a spirit the artist himself did much to help maintain. (© Mrs J. C. Robinson by kind permission of the proprietor and Pollinger Limited/ILN Picture Library)

'Bluffing the Periscope', W. Heath Robinson, *The Sketch*, 27 June 1917

Caption: *Taking cover from U-Boats: Hints for bathers unnecessarily nervous about submarines off shore.*

More silliness in the face of adversity from Heath Robinson, whose suggestions for headwear designed to fool lurking U-boats verge on the ridiculous. But U-boats were a very real threat. German submarine crews were ordered to torpedo anything that might be carrying supplies or troops to enemy shores. They were remarkably successful, sinking 227 ships in 1915 and, infamously, the passenger liner the *Lusitania* the following year. (© Mrs J. C. Robinson by kind permission of the proprietor and Pollinger Limited/ILN Picture Library)

'Dutiful as Usual', J. H. Dowd, *The Bystander*, 1 December 1915

Caption: *Imperturbable James: 'I don't know whether you would care to see them, sir, but the Zeppelins have come.'*

The butler's calm, unruffled delivery of this rather terrifying piece of news is British comedy at its deadpan best (J. H. Dowd was a regular for *Punch* from 1906). Zeppelins, huge monsters of the sky, held a chilling fascination for the population. They could be vulnerable in bad weather conditions, and British anti-aircraft fire successfully shot down or damaged around two-thirds of the German Zeppelin fleet. The first Zeppelin to be brought down by the Royal Flying Corps was the L21, in Cuffley, Hertfordshire on 3 September 1916, winning Lieutenant William Leefe Robinson the Victoria Cross. Despite its drawbacks, the Zeppelin was still responsible for 550 civilian deaths during the course of the war.

'Zepp! Zepp! Hurray!', Lewis Baumer, *The Sketch*, 31 May 1916

Caption: *The Optimist (on the morning after the raid): 'Well, you always wanted a rock garden, didn't you, dear?'*

Lewis Baumer excelled at drawing 'polite society' in all its manifestations, but unlike H. M. Bateman who drew his inspiration from the same genre, Baumer's humour is gentler and complements his warm, lively drawing style. The cheery optimism of this man, while his wife and daughter peer into a fresh bomb crater in the garden with bewildered consternation, is typical of Baumer's comic timing. Quite coincidentally, it forecasts an unfortunate event that beset Baumer during more bombing raids, this time during World War II when his late-Georgian house, studio and garden in St John's Wood was rendered uninhabitable by a bomb in September 1940. The house was certified a 'total loss' by the War Damage Commission and Baumer was only able to recoup his losses by the sale of his garden after the war.

A FAMILIAR SCENE SOMEWHERE IN THE CITY

ZEPPELIN-EYE VIEW OF THE SAME SCENE

'How to Hoodwink the Zeppelins: The Latest Device for Disguising London', Harry Rountree, *The Bystander*, 9 December 1914

A cunning idea by Harry Rountree transforms London streets into an agricultural landscape, at least from the viewpoint of a Zeppelin pilot. Rountree (1878–1950) was sought after for his anthropomorphic animal pictures, which were regularly used in children's books, so it is no surprise to see him incorporating some farmyard friends into this illustration. During the war, he served as a Captain with the Royal Engineers.

'When the Raider Drops In: Hints for Householders', W. Heath Robinson, *The Bystander*, 4 July 1917

Despite the advantage of its island status, Britain felt that the German army was perilously close. In 1917, the British army demanded 100,000 men a month in order to mount a spring offensive on the Western Front and two divisions from the home army were sent to France. This worried the home army's commanders who were convinced at least 500,000 men were needed to resist a German invasion. With the absence of a sufficient home guard, Heath Robinson's advice for a family discovering a German raider may have come in handy. (© Mrs J. C. Robinson by kind permission of the proprietor and Pollinger Limited/ILN Picture Library)

'But – A Rumour!', H. H. Harris, *The Sketch*, 16 January 1918

Caption: *Not a 'take cover' warning – merely an early-morning butter rumour in suburbia*

Not a Zeppelin raid, but a rumour that butter is available for sale, provokes a stampede among inhabitants of a sleepy suburb. A long campaign by the government, which attempted to re-educate and persuade people to eat less and grow more, failed to prevent food shortages and panic buying. Queues were a regular feature of a housewife's daily shop, and many people suspected shop owners were reserving food for their preferred customers, leaving very little for those who had been patiently queuing in line. The problem was compounded by munitions workers, newly financially solvent and not about to start denying themselves a few little luxuries. Nationwide rationing was eventually introduced in April 1918.

'Profit-tears', Fred Buchanan, *The Bystander*, 13 November 1918

Caption: *The Profiteer (lamenting the shortage of raw material): 'Yes, this would'a been a good war if we could 'ave 'ad it in peace-time'*

While the majority of the population grappled with ever-decreasing food supplies, for some the war meant vast profits, so it is unsurprising that Fred Buchanan draws his profiteers with waistlines to match their wallets. Inevitably, the iron, coal, shipbuilding and engineering industries saw an increase in profits during the war years, and farmers did well too, benefiting from the scarcity of imported food. As a rule, the government turned a blind eye to profiteering providing supplies remained constant. Lord Devonport was well aware of the problem, admitting to Lloyd George that 'profiteering is rife in every commodity…and the masses are being exploited right and left.'

'Forward!', Wilmot Lunt, *The Sketch*, 29 September 1915

Caption: *The Grocer (to the new hand): 'And always put in the date these war-tax times; so that you can add it up with the rest of the bill'*

During the war, duties and licences were introduced or increased across a varying range of commodities including sugar, tea, coffee, beer and matches. Wilmot Lunt's cartoon not only reflects the rising prices that resulted from this indirect taxation, but also conveys the mistrust of shopkeepers who were often suspected of profiting from the war.

'Picked from the Woods: Preparing Seeds for the Raspberry Jam Rations', W. Heath Robinson, *The Bystander*, 20 November 1918

The outrageous inefficiency and misuse of resources in Heath Robinson's raspberry jam factory could almost be symbolic of the petty nit-picking accordant with food rationing. Seeds (to add authenticity to jam rations) are wood chips – shaped, measured, polished, disinfected, flavoured and stained all in the finest Heath Robinson tradition of solemn convolution. (© Mrs J. C. Robinson by kind permission of the proprietor and Pollinger Limited/ILN Picture Library)

'The Economy Campaign', Alfred Leete, *The Bystander*, 15 March 1916

Caption: *The Brown-Jones family's practical way of tackling the situation*

In the new climate of thrift, this particular family economises by eating pets, fashioning a pram out of a soapbox and drowning the family dog! Hopefully few civilians were reduced to taking quite such drastic or brutal measures, although with the scarcity of meat, it's probable that only a small proportion of pet rabbits survived the war. Diets fluctuated depending on what was available when. Potatoes often replaced bread as a source of carbohydrate while lentils provided a cheaper source of protein. The allotment system germinated during World War I and everyone was encouraged to grow their own food. Even the flowerbeds of Buckingham Palace were turned over to become vegetable plots.

'A Nasal Reconnaissance: Discovering German spies in Tottenham Court Road',
W. Heath Robinson, *The Sketch*, 26 August 1914

The 35,000 Germans living in Britain at the outbreak of war made up the third largest immigrant group in the country. Out of this, only 22 were identified as real spies, but distrust and fear spread like wildfire through the population, with the flames of suspicion fanned by newspapers such as the *Daily Mail*, which suggested demanding to see the passport of any waiter appearing to be German but claiming to be Swiss. Even thousands of pigeons did not escape suspicion; many were shot on sight in 1914, thought to be carriers of messages from spies. Heath Robinson pictures this atmosphere with his usual dry humour as three policeman attempt to lure a German from his flat with his nation's staple food – sausages. (© Mrs J. C. Robinson by kind permission of the proprietor and Pollinger Limited/ILN Picture Library)

'The East Coast is So Bracing!', James H. Thorpe, *The Tatler*, 17 February 1915
When the East Coast suffered a coastal bombardment in January 1915, the opportunity to produce a satirical homage to John Hassall's famous 'Skegness is So Bracing' poster (originally designed in 1908) must have been irresistible. This time round, Thorpe's old salt is not quite so carefree, and Skegness's bracing qualities are of a distinctly more menacing variety!

Above: 'Zeppelingitis', 'Rif', *The Bystander*, 28 October 1914
Caption: *The Editors of 'The Bystander', 'The Graphic' and 'Daily Graphic' tender their deep regrets to the elderly gentleman shown in the picture for having caused him to be unnecessarily alarmed on his way home from the City the other evening*
Opposite: 'Wait Your Turn', Douglas Mackenzie, *The Bystander*, 31 May 1916
Caption: *Hungry Club Members: A Sad Result of the Paper Famine*

The *Graphic* and *The Bystander* were located in Tallis Street, a small street running parallel to the Thames and bustling Fleet Street. On a dark night, with gas lighting extinguished and searchlights swooping across the sky, the day's delivery of paper bears a startling resemblance to a hovering Zeppelin.

But the abundance of paper in 1914 would become a rarity in 1918. Imports of raw materials and paper from overseas were restricted and soon it became a scarce commodity. A notice in *The Bystander* in June 1918 under the title, 'The Importance of Paper', instructed readers who came across instances of waste of paper to write to the Paper Controller at 23, Buckingham Gate, SW1. A report of the 19th General Meeting of The Illustrated London News & Sketch Limited in *The Times* in March 1918 focused on the company's squeezed profits due to the paper shortage. Charles Ingram is quoted: 'We have not been able to show you such

a good balance-sheet this year as we did last year, but it was quite beyond the power of the board to obviate this. The paper question has affected us most seriously…and has cost us thousands of pounds extra.' Another member of the board, Mr G. J. Maddick, pointed out that, considering the circumstances, the profit of £28,000 was very respectable, adding that he hoped at the war's end 'to retain our popularity and friendship of our readers, and we shall be well on towards the prosperity that we have enjoyed in former years'.

It was a paradoxically difficult time for the press. Despite increased circulation (for dailies as well as illustrated newspapers) and advertising revenue, the cost of paper was quite crippling and some magazines failed to survive the last months of the war. *The Illustrated War News*, a spin-off magazine from the *ILN*, had to close, but all the others survived, even if, as in the case of *The Bystander*, disgruntled club members might have to wait their turn to read the latest issue!

OH! MR. McKENNA !!

(A feature of the War Budget is the taxation of foreign-made hats)

Above: 'Up-to-date Economy – Combination Gown for War-Time', Lewis Baumer,
The Bystander, **2 February 1916**

The war forced the fashionable to be resourceful, and this two-in-one dress, the suggestion of Lewis Baumer, would seamlessly take the wearer from day to night. In 1918, there was an attempt to introduce a National Standard Dress, a plain and rather ugly utility garment designed to cover all sartorial eventualities (even its usefulness as a nightgown was guaranteed). It was the subject of an exhibition of war economy dress held at the Grafton Galleries during August of that year, with daily lectures by Mrs Allan Hawkey, the inventor. Such a garment was unlikely to be taken up by stylish readers of *The Bystander.*

Right: 'Oh! Mr. McKenna!!', Mabel Lucie Attwell, *The Bystander,* **29 September 1915**

In his budget speech on 21 September 1915, Reginald McKenna, the Chancellor of the Exchequer, announced a tax of 33 per cent, known as the 'McKenna duties', on the import of foreign luxury goods, including motor cars, motorcycles, cinema films, clocks, musical instruments and hats. The measures were partly to 'adjust the balance of international exchange' and partly to 'effect domestic economies'. *The Bystander*'s editor, Vivian Carter, a free trade exponent, took the opportunity to voice his views with the help of Mabel Lucie Attwell's heartbroken hat fanatic.

'Christmas in the home – of a Peace-Crank (Toys supplied by relatives)', Bert Thomas, *The Bystander*, 24 November 1915

Quite unfettered by today's political correctness, toy manufacturers during the war produced a range of shockingly accurate miniature weapons and tanks, such as the 'anti-aircraft Maxim Gun, beautifully made in solid brass' available for 10s 9d. A variety of such war-themed toys has awoken a primitive aggression in the home of this 'peace-crank' (note the disdainful terminology). A letter to *The Times* in December 1918 echoes his concern: 'Sir, – It is somewhat distressing at a time when we are talking so much about permanent peace for future generations that our children should be fed mentally by means of toys associated with killing and destruction…[in] a manner to consider war and the military life as the noblest and best thing on earth…'

'It's an Ill Wind', Dudley Tennant, *The Bystander*, 6 December 1918

Caption: *Angelina: 'I'm so glad that horrid Brunhilde and her Fritz won't be at any of our parties this year!'*

Before the war, the majority of children's toys in British stores were of German origin, with names like Steiff, Armand Marseille and Gebruder Bing synonymous with quality and good value. Even if there had not been a ban on German imports, the nation would certainly not have tolerated German toys and was concerned over reports that German-made toys were making it into the country under the guise of being American. The popular Kewpie doll's production was moved to France and Belgium from Germany during the war, and people bought toys made by British manufacturers (including those employing disabled soldiers). By 1920, German toys were back in the shops again.

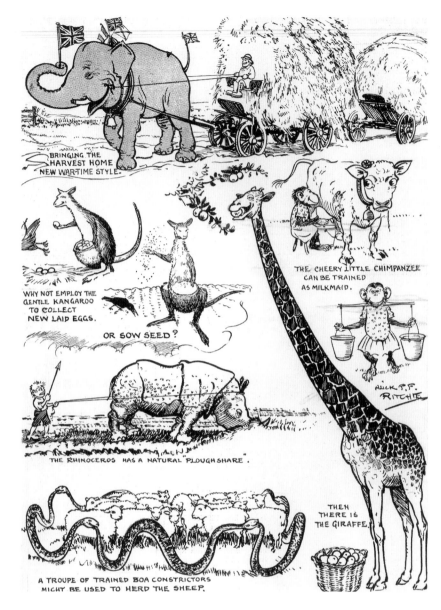

'Monday Morning's Mistakes: Daylight Saving at Slocum-in-the-Hole', H. M. Brock,
The Bystander, 24 May 1916

Daylight saving was first suggested by William Willett in 1907, who sadly died in 1915 before
the bill was passed in May 1916. Germany introduced daylight saving a few weeks before
Britain and once it was implemented, even the reluctant farmers could see the benefits.
H. M. Brock was a prolific illustrator who worked almost entirely in pen and ink.

'Freak Friends for Farmers: Some Hints for the New Minister of Agriculture', Alick P.
F. Ritchie, *The Bystander*, 12 July 1916

Elephants were in fact used on farms in some parts of the country during the war, and *The
Illustrated War News* even carried a photograph of an elephant pulling loads in Sheffield. They
must have been a bizarre sight. I am particularly fond of Ritchie's 'cheery little chimpanzee'
acting as a milkmaid!

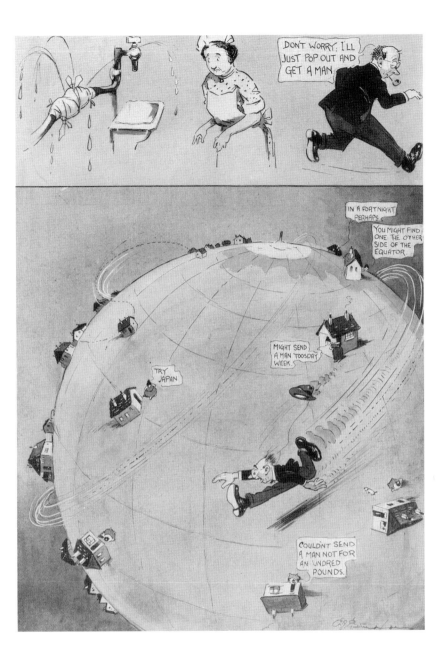

'War-Time Studdys! VI. – A Horrible Realisation of the Shortage of Labour', George Studdy, *The Sketch*, 10 May 1916

Kitchener's Army competed with industry at home for manpower, and the irony of Kitchener's success was that there was insufficient labour to produce the munitions and the equipment his million plus recruits required. The introduction of conscription in 1916 led to yet more domestic havoc, and as George Studdy's cartoon suggests, anyone wanting an 'odd-job man' to carry out minor household repairs would have been hard pressed to find one. (© George Studdy/ILN Picture Library)

'*The Illustrated London News* Christmas Number', Cyrus Cuneo, *The Illustrated London News*, November 1916

This family toasting the portrait of an absent father at Christmas was painted by Cyrus Cincinnato Cuneo (1879–1916), one of the *ILN*'s regular artists. His subjects are comfortably middle class, the table of their softly lit parlour looks plentiful and the children are well-dressed, the son in the ubiquitous sailor suit.

The Blue Pencil

Reporting & Censorship

On 6 August 1914, the Press Bureau was established by the First Lord of the Admiralty, Winston Churchill, who stressed it would provide 'a steady stream of trustworthy information supplied both by the War Office and the Admiralty which can be given to the press'. Presided over by F. E. Smith (coincidentally Churchill's best friend), the Bureau's publicity-generating machinery seemed regularly to run dry of news, and Fleet Street – quickly realising that the agency's main concern was with censorship, rather than publicity – soon began to label it the 'Suppress Bureau'.

In truth, at first there was very little news for the Bureau to suppress, as Lord Kitchener refused to allow any war correspondents near the Front. When the British Expeditionary Force embarked for France, it was not reported until three days after the event, and the opportunity to write some glowing headlines about what was a relatively positive event was missed, frustrating newspaper editors beyond belief. In the absence of any real news, the Bureau instead busied itself with upholding the government's more extreme regulations. Weather reports were censored, in the belief that such information was useful to the enemy, and even chess columns – a natural conduit for coded messages – were suspended.

Censorship had a twofold purpose. The first was to prevent valuable information getting into enemy hands; the second, unequivocally, was to keep the public in a state of ignorance. Some papers exercised a form of self-censorship, knowing the effect that reporting the truth might have on the country's morale. F. E. Smith's successor, Sir Stanley Buckmaster, freely admitted that he sought to control information that would 'unduly depress our people'. Ignorance was not necessarily bliss and this patronising line

'Passed by the Censor', Edwin Morrow, *The Bystander*, 16 August 1916

Caption: *Officers of the ___ Battn. ___ Regt., who took part in a recent advance in ___. Reading from left to right (back row): Lieut.___, Lieut.___, Sec.-Lieut.___, Lieut.___, Sec.-Lieut.___. Front row: Capt.___, Lieut.-Col.___, Major___, and Capt.___*

The Defence of the Realm Act (DORA) gave the government sweeping control over the press, leading to the establishment of the Press Bureau in the early weeks of the war, whose remit was to spoon-feed expurgated news to the media. Exponents of press freedom felt the Bureau's regulations could be unnecessarily severe and verging on the ridiculous, a fact that Edwin Morrow's cartoon seeks to emphasise.

EDWIN MORROW—

left a bad taste in the mouths of those members of the press with integrity. Lord Rothermere admitted 'We're telling lies, we know we're telling lies, we daren't tell the truth.'

By the spring of 1915, the Press Bureau's chief censor was E. T. Cook, formerly an editor of the *Daily News*, the *Pall Mall Gazette* and the *Westminster Gazette*. He was a man known for a rather dull and literal grasping of the information that passed through his hands, but, as a journalist, he did at least understand that it was far better to harness the power of the (largely patriotic) press, than to subject it to dogmatic intransigence. It was a wise move. By spring 1915, the first accredited correspondents were appointed, among them Percival Philips for *The Daily Express* and Battersby for *The Morning Post*. But although the newshounds made it to France, it was far from plain sailing when they got there. Accompanied everywhere by press officers, there were still constraints on what they could report.

Fortunately for weekly 'glossies' such as the *ILN* magazines, the Press Bureau's main concern seemed to be with controlling the handful of opinion-forming daily newspapers, and although it would be naïve to believe magazines like *The Sketch* or *The Bystander* did not come under scrutiny too (most pictures have the line 'Passed by Censor'), it seems that perhaps they were shown more leniency than the dailies. Add the fact that many pictures originally published in the *ILN* magazines were then licensed out for use in other publications and reproduced as postcards, and it is clear that the influence of these magazines extended far beyond the upper middle-class readership for which they were originally intended.

Unsurprisingly, among the *ILN* magazines it was *The Bystander* that took a stand on the subject of overbearing censorship, with its cheeky brand of humour. But it could only push the boundaries so far and its maverick approach even led to a legal prosecution and the dismissal of its editor, Vivian

Carter, in February 1916 after a particular picture of a drunken soldier, drawn by an officer of the 10th West Yorkshire Regiment, was deemed 'a gross libel on the Forces of his Majesty'. It speaks volumes about the atmosphere of paranoia as well as of the far-reaching influence of illustrated magazines that the case earned such publicity.

The Illustrated London News along with *The Sphere* and *The Graphic* was much more likely obediently to toe the line. The *ILN* sent the likes of Frederic Villiers and Julius Price to the Front, its aim to present a faithful representation of the war in France to its readers. The 'lighter' magazines instead seem to echo popular preoccupations. It might be presumptuous to suggest that *The Bystander* and others spoke for the common man, but it is clear the jokes were those shared by civilians at home, as well as by soldiers abroad, a policy that sealed the magazine's popularity. Meanwhile, in response to the limitations imposed by the censor, humorous artists decided to turn the tables and draw from experience, depicting themselves in inspirational turmoil all because of the state's rationing of suitable ideas.

Of course, censorship was not limited solely to the press. The extreme restrictions imposed on men serving at the Front meant that often, letters home gave few more details other than, 'I am well' and 'Give Billy a kiss from his dad.' Divulging details of location or anything close to military information was strictly forbidden; a state of affairs that artists treated with their customary good-natured sarcasm.

It says something for the limitless enterprise and diplomacy of many magazine illustrators that their work continued unabated, despite the censor's blue pencil. Pictures had a magically evasive advantage over prose. They could carry intangible messages that could be unlocked by those 'in the know' but were too obviously conveyed by words. In war, a picture really could be worth a thousand words.

'The Order In Council', 'Nibs', *The Bystander,* **10 May 1916**

Caption: *'Chorus of 'Free' Press – 'Hush! Hush!! Hush!!! Here comes the Bogey Man.'*

Prime Minister Herbert Asquith rises up like a spectre of doom in this satirical piece by 'Nibs', sending various newspapers scurrying in panic with his ghoulish presence. Heads of the Press Bureau might come and go, but through the first two years of the war, Asquith remained the censorial constant. The Prime Minister noted that 'the newspapers complain we keep them on a starvation diet', and advised Churchill to 'season any news with the appropriate condiments' in order to keep complaints at bay. 'Nibs' is obviously a pseudonym – perhaps anonymity was best for such an outspoken illustration.

'That Queer "Censation" – Felt by "Bystander" artists throughout the censor's reign',
Helen McKie, *The Bystander,* **29 January 1919**

 Helen McKie's post-war picture sat opposite a rather tongue-in-cheek piece by 'Blanche', *The Bystander*'s weekly columnist, who wrote that she had rather liked leading a life of subterfuge and intrigue with all its romantic possibilities, mourning that 'life will be a trifle dull' without the censor. McKie worked on the staff of *The Bystander* for 14 years from 1915 to 1929 and was well placed to record the frustrations felt by artists during the World War I period. Interestingly, this monstrous censor has the same spectral appearance as Asquith in the previous illustration.

'A Study in Creation', T. Mackenzie, *The Bystander*, 14 October 1914

Caption: *The Editor and Staff of a Daily Newspaper Search a Censored Telegram for News.*

There is a distinctly 'Heath Robinson' tone to this illustration by T. Mackenzie, which shows the rather oddball staff of a daily newspaper using a variety of optical instruments to detect news in a censored missive from France. When war broke out, a number of correspondents were already in France and were able to send through reports. However, Kitchener quickly clamped down on any unauthorised correspondents; some were even arrested. By mid-August, news was sparse, leading editors to complain, as well as to exaggerate any reports they did receive.

'People We Don't Envy: No. IV. – The humorous artist who turns up his funniest joke on a day when there happens to be bad news from the war', G. E. Studdy, *The Bystander*, 17 February 1915

Studdy's rather piteous artist finds his comic genius has peaked at an unfortunate time. It also suggests the delicate balance required of magazine editors, who had quickly to learn how to gauge public opinion and to present bad news in a way that would not alienate their readership. Opinion for its own sake was not always welcome, as *The Daily Mail* discovered when Lord Northcliffe dared to suggest the shortage of armaments was the fault of the popular Lord Kitchener. Within a week, its circulation had plummeted by one million. (© George Studdy/ILN Picture Library)

'Sensible of the Censor', unattributed, *The Bystander*, 19 July 1916

Caption: *'My Dear Mother, — Just a line to let you know I am quite well as it leaves me at present, but I am not allowed to say so, — I remain your loving son, Walter'*

Newspapers were not alone in being victims of censorship. Most letters home from soldiers or sailors had to pass through a censor, leaving men with the unenviable task of writing up a selection of inane news and being forced to omit the most affecting experiences.

'Supra-Normal', Bruce Bairnsfather, *The Bystander*, 27 September 1916

Caption: *Captain Mills-Bomme's temperature cracks the thermometer on seeing his recent daring exploits described as 'On our right there is nothing to report' (He and his battalion had merely occupied three lines of German trenches, and held them through a storm of heavy Lyddite for forty-eight hours)*

Incandescent with rage, Bairnsfather's wounded soldier highlights the chasm of understanding between the British press and those who were experiencing the war first-hand, not least the tendency of newspaper editors to sensationalise some stories and file others in the waste paper basket. World War I was characterised by few 'battles' in the traditional sense, but more by a series of attacks and incidents, many of which could be missed, especially if not included in despatches. At least this wounded officer appears to be in safe hands now.

'K. R. and A. I. (Illustrated). No. 2 – Purchase of Foreign Literature', Arthur Watts, *The Bystander*, 7 February 1917

Caption: '*A sum not exceeding £5 may be spent. . .upon the purchase of such literature for use in foreign languages as may be deemed suitable and necessary*'.

Three sailors enjoying *La Vie Parisienne* in the full knowledge that this type of literature is not the sort recommended in the *King's Regulations* and *Admiralty Instructions*. *La Vie Parisienne*, often described as the French equivalent to *The Sketch* (although certainly more risqué), would have been widely available to soldiers. Certainly it seems weekly glossies had a genuine part to play in lifting the spirits. One soldier correspondent in *The Bystander* wrote, 'The Weekly Illustrateds are as Gin at a mothers' meeting to us here'.

'Reported Missing', Second Lieutenant C. E. B. Bernard, *The Bystander*, 26 January 1916

This particular cartoon plunged *The Bystander* into serious trouble, leading to a prosecution at Mansion House in London on 18 February under the *Defence of the Realm Act*. *The Times* called it, 'a disgusting representation without any humour', while the prosecutor noted that, as well as being a 'gross libel on the Forces of his Majesty' and 'likely to prejudice recruiting and discipline because it was a drawing by an officer of a private', the magazine's circulation abroad, even in Germany, gave it a more serious aspect. A week later, there was another libel case over a photograph in which an officer at a recruiting rally felt he was misrepresented and Vivian Carter was dismissed. The publishers were fined £100, and Carter and the artist were each fined £50. Considering the morale-boosting effects of many *Bystander* cartoons up to that point, especially those of Bruce Bairnsfather, it seems harsh that Carter was given his notice. The cartoon was ill judged but, to our eyes, seems relatively harmless.

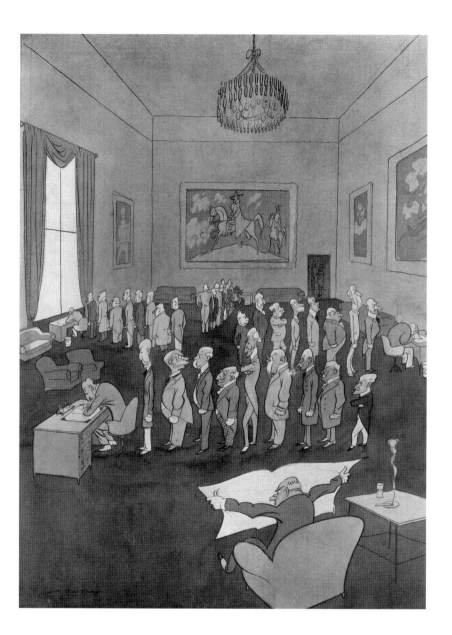

'I Remember that in 1870 – Parading for writing-to-the-papers: A London Club in war-time', H. M. Bateman, *The Sketch*, 14 October 1914

H. M. Bateman was the undisputed master of lampooning polite society and in this picture, a long line of ex-Colonels and 'disgusted of Tunbridge Wells' types line up to write to the newspapers. An older generation of armchair commentators, keen to offer views based on a very different type of warfare from the previous century, was a particular gripe for many serving soldiers. (© H. M. Bateman Designs Limited/ILN Picture Library)

'No Joke!', Frank Reynolds, *The Sketch*, 26 April 1916

Caption: *The Humourist (who has exhausted his War jokes): 'It's really very tantalising. I've got some lovely stunts on Peace – if they'd only declare it!'*

Sadly, this artist would have to eke out his war jokes for another two and a half years before his 'stunts' on peace could be published. Frank Reynolds speaks for all illustrators about the endless problem of coming up with new ideas, although Reynolds himself was rarely short of inspiration.

Carrying On

Women & War

The majority of men who marched off to war left behind them empty office desks, unploughed fields and conductor-less buses. Fate had suddenly opened up the floodgates of opportunity for women, and they seized their chance with both hands.

How much the war actually played a part in aiding women's struggle for equality remains a subject of debate. Certainly, those employed in war work, specifically munitions, earned far less than their male counterparts had done before the war, and most lost their jobs once the war was over. Women knew they could help the war effort above and beyond their traditional roles, but it was not so easy to persuade the male establishment, who still firmly believed the old adage that a woman's place was in the home. Many educated ladies, with no other outlet for their talents, energetically threw themselves into voluntary and charitable work, but there was a widespread reluctance to encourage women to take up more militant roles that might somehow involve them in the dirty business of war. Dr Elsie Inglis famously visited the War Office in 1914 offering to raise an ambulance unit but was gruffly told by an official, 'My good lady, go home and sit still.' But Dr Inglis, and thousands of other women, did not sit still.

The enthusiasm and patriotic surge engendered by the war did not just affect men and the female population was anxious to do its bit. Literally hundreds of organisations, the majority of them entirely voluntary, sprang up with the express purpose to answer the country's call – whether that was by knitting socks for soldiers, or driving ambulances under shell fire. Patriarchal resistance was such that it was not until 1917 that the Women's Army Auxiliary Corps (WAAC), and later the Women's Royal Naval Service

'First Aid', Wilmot Lunt, *The Bystander*, 6 June 1917
This picture, originally a double page spread in *The Bystander*, was reproduced again in *The Strand* magazine to accompany a profile on Wilmot Lunt and must have been one of his favourites. The comic insinuation, that a WAAC girl driver is more concerned with her appearance than with the car (containing an officer) she has just crashed, is a harmless gag but still perpetuates the notion that women were preoccupied with frivolity. The WAAC personnel were not allowed to use the title 'officer'. Instead, they were known as 'officials'; NCOs were 'forewomen' and the rank and file were known as 'workers'. The WAAC uniform was khaki, with a full skirt considered daringly short (12 inches above ground). The round, brown felt hat this driver is so keen to arrange was known as a 'baby boy' due to its resemblance to school children's hats.

(WRNS) and the Women's Royal Air Force (WRAF), were founded, branches of the armed forces whose purpose was to provide backup to the combatants, both at home and abroad. The tasks were multifarious; women became cooks, cleaners, mechanics, drivers, telephonists and clerks. In truth, many of these jobs were menial and dirty, and the pay was poor, yet women often left jobs in factories to join 'the army', lured by suggestion of glamour and excitement, even if very few ever got anywhere near a ship or the front line.

But there was no arguing against the importance of this contribution. The British army practically ran on horses, and so the Women's Forage Corps, responsible for baling hay and driving horse-drawn transport, played a pivotal role, while the Lady Instructors' Signal Company (part of the Women's Volunteer Reserve, WVR), which was expert in communication, taught officers to use Morse code, semaphore flags and flashlights. The work might be hard – it might even be tedious – but the satisfaction came from being part of a national effort.

The class divisions that underpinned the British forces were mirrored in their female equivalent. Most of these organisations were voluntary and the majority of women were drawn from 'good families'. Some not only expected their members to work for free but were also expensive to join – the WVR, with its uniform at £2, was only possible for the affluent few. The Women's Land Army tended to attract more middle-class girls, drawn to a rose-tinted rustic idyll populated by long-lashed dairy cows and perfectly formed haystacks. Working class women, well aware of how poor the wages were for such back-breaking work, shied away from the countryside and opted for the munitions factories, where earnings were far more than they were used to. The First Aid Nursing Yeomanry (FANY), a rather select group of upper-class women which worked with the Red Cross, mainly as ambulance drivers, was a great favourite of the *ILN* magazines, whose readership came from the same stock. The presence of women in what had formerly been male strongholds naturally led to public moral concern, not just about 'munitionettes', who, suddenly solvent, were thought to fritter away their money on stockings and drink, but about the free and easy fraternisation between men and women in the armed forces. The fears were unfounded, with far fewer pregnancies than there would have been at home. The WRNS rose above it all, maintaining their reputation for being 'perfect ladies'.

The war saw the image of the vapid Edwardian lady give way to the plucky, can-do attitude of the Voluntary Aid Detachment (VAD) or Women's Women's Army Auxiliary Corps. Women in uniform or munitions girls full of sass and sauce made ideal subjects, both photographically and artistically, and combined the two aims of the magazine artist – to paint what was current, and to paint what would please. Illustrators were able, for the first time, to portray the fairer sex in far more positive and proactive roles. It is unsurprising that after the war the artists who painted these pictures created on canvas the confident flapper girls, of whom the working women of World War I had been forebears. Artists such as Edmund Blampied and Reginald Higgins would soon be artistic protagonists of the genre.

The female contribution to the war effort was immense. Over 100,000 women joined the forces' support services, 300,000 worked in munitions and countless others in volunteer units. It was a massive and assiduous effort that paid dividends not just in Britain's eventual victory, but over the next decade when women won the right they so richly deserved – to be able to vote.

'Going to be Accepted', Douglas Mackenzie, *The Bystander*, 6 December 1916

Caption: *Woman Power in Tallis Street — What we may expect when all — !*

Douglas Mackenzie's apocalyptic view of *The Bystander* offices, with an entirely female staff, is a humorous and possibly rather nervous comment on the increasing number of women in the workplace. The scene is completed by the cigarette, a mark of nonchalant (and rather shocking) sophistication, in between the lips of the art editor as she inspects one soldier-artist's work.

'The Summer Girl, 1917', Edwin Morrow, *The Bystander*, 6 June 1917

Caption: *Far from the hill-side, far from the sea, Far from the homes where they'd love to be—*
Tied to their desks (for the men are gone), Maud, Gertie, and Mabel are 'carrying on'

In the decade from 1911 to 1921, the number of women employed in clerical work rose from 124,000 to 591,000. During the war, as male clerks left their desks to answer the country's call, women were needed to fill their places, or, to paraphrase Lieutenant General Sir Henry Lawson, do the 'soft jobs'. Various fast-track training schemes run by councils ensured a steady supply, but by August 1916, *The Times* reported a 'dearth of women clerks': 'Tens of thousands of women have come into business life since the war began, and it may be that the reservoir of suitable material is being drained more rapidly than it can be fed from the training colleges and special classes… At one time Whitehall officials could pick and choose their clerks and the majority of those engaged were of an adaptable age – from 20 to 30 – but an intelligent girl of 17 without experience can now find a place, and middle-aged women need no longer think they are not wanted.' The presence of army officers in Edwin Morrow's picture probably means these women are part of the WAAC, which had been formed in January 1917.

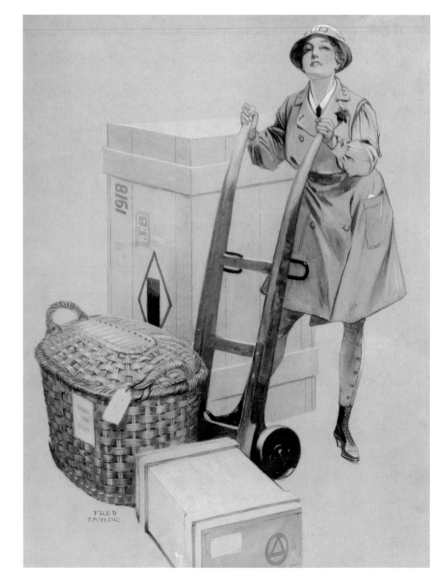

'Whitehall-marked – Winnie – of the War Office', Reginald Higgins, *The Tatler*,
9 October 1918

The 'new woman' was Reginald Higgins' trademark. As the war years rolled into the 1920s, Higgins' girls epitomised the desirable androgyny of the era, with their Eton crops, gramophone records, golf clubs and cigarettes. In this Higgins picture, 'Winnie' cuts a fashionable figure emerging from an office in Whitehall where no doubt she's been typing and filing. For the upper-class readers of *The Tatler*, this was probably just the sort of job they might hope for.

'Carrying On: No. 3 – The Railway Girl', Fred Taylor, *The Bystander*, 19 June 1918

Fred Taylor created a number of colour illustrations for *The Bystander* under the title 'Carrying On' – a phrase that summed up the Home Front, specifically the female effort throughout the war. As well as the railway porter shown here, he painted an RAF girl, a window-cleaner, a Whitehall office worker and a WAAC driver, a range of employment that implies each and every working woman was helping the war effort regardless of who she was, or what she did. Fred Taylor was a talented poster artist and was commissioned to produce a number of designs for the LNER railway company during the 1920s and 30s. He continued to use his artistic skills in World War II in the naval camouflage unit.

'Wonderful Woman', Edmund Blampied, *The Sketch*, supplement

Caption: *She used to scream at the sight of a mouse; now she faces shell-fire with a smile*

This wonderfully positive tribute by Edmund Blampied admires women's courageous progress in the face of war, from frailty to bravery. The women who joined VADs or the ready-trained units, such as the Queen Alexandra Imperial Nursing Corps sent to France, were predominantly from middle- or upper-class backgrounds. Most had led sheltered lives in comfortable surroundings and would have been quite unprepared for what they were about to face. (© Estate of Edmund Blampied/ILN Picture Library)

'Little Sister', Raphael Kirchner, *The Sketch* Christmas Number, 1915

According to Raphael Kirchner, even nurses are allowed to powder their noses. Nurses were regularly referred to in celestial vernacular as 'Angels of Mercy' or 'Ministering Angels', a fantasy that prevailed throughout the war, aided by the religious air conveyed by most uniforms. Kirchner adds a sexual allure to the image with a dust of powder and a glimpse of chequered stockings.

IF GRETEL, WITHOUT TELLING ANY ONE, CHOSE TO MAKE SHELLS.—

—WAS IT LIKELY THAT MARY WOULD SIT BY WITH FOLDED ARMS?—

—OR THAT MARIANNE WOULD NOT GET TO WORK?—

—AND, WITH RUSSIA AND ITALY GIVING A HAND ALSO, HERE WE ARE WITH PLENTY OF MUNITIONS.

'A "Field-Day" with Giles', Edmund Blampied, *The Bystander*, 26 July 1916
Edmund Blampied's jaunty land girl projects the wholesome, rural idyll the government hoped would entice women to volunteer to work the land. Agricultural labour was tough and poorly paid, and several voluntary organisations, including the Board of Agriculture's Women's National Land Service Corps, the Women's Defence Relief Corps and the Women's Legion failed to drum up the numbers required. The Women's Land Army, formed in 1917, was still only able to attract an additional 16,000 women. The jovial Farmer Giles is also at odds with reality; many farmers were reluctant to accept women, often preferring male pensioners. (© Estate of Edmund Blampied/ILN Picture Library)

'Vanities of Valdes: The Munitioneers', 'VAL', *The Sketch*, 11 August 1915
This resounding message of Allied female solidarity shows 'Mary' of Britain and 'Marianne' of France, who, together with Russia and Italy will make enough shells to overcome 'Gretel' of Germany and her stealthy war preparations. The munitionettes were integral to the war effort, and it was vital that the Allied munitions factories should out-produce the enemy.

'Munitions', Hutton Mitchell, *The Bystander*, 17 May 1916

Caption: *'I want to leave nex' week, mum, I'm agoin' to work on munitions'*
'Well, Mary, if you drop things there as often as you've done here, you won't be long in your new place'

This cartoon by Hutton Mitchell, which is very much in the *Punch* tradition, depicts a common scenario created by the war. The 'servant problem' became very real for middle- and upper-class homeowners, who found butlers and menservants joining up while the temptation of higher wages at the munitions factories lured maids away from service. One officer's wife admitted, 'Neither my Mother, sister or myself had ever done any serious housework or cooking of any kind, so it was an entirely new experience to be confronted with meals to cook, rooms to clean, and required an entirely new mental adjustment.' Hutton Mitchell also illustrated the Billy Bunter stories, written by Frank Richards and published in *The Magnet*.

'Female Munitions Workers', Fortunino Matania, *The Sphere*, 24 June 1916

The grand scale of shell production is the essence of this staggeringly cavernous munitions factory created by Fortunino Matania, with the humming machines seeming to disappear into infinity. Munitions workers earned relatively high wages but there was a price to pay. There were dangerous side-effects associated with the chemicals, and all those working with TNT developed yellow faces and hands, earning them the nickname of 'canaries'. The symptoms could be debilitating, even fatal at times, while the danger of working among explosives, especially in combination with enemy air attacks, could be deadly. Matania regularly used members of his family as models for his work. This picture features Goldie (Ellen Jane Goldsack), who became Matania's second wife in 1960.

'Now that Women are Doing Men's Jobs', George Studdy, *The Sketch*, 1 December 1915
Pretty girls playing Father Christmas was a repeated theme throughout the war, but, having been generated by a male artist's brush, they unsurprisingly seem more concerned with flashing their legs and smiling at the reader than donning a fake beard. (© George Studdy/ILN Picture Library)

'Shades of our Grandmothers!', Euan Lyne, *The Bystander* front cover, 18 August 1915
The image of women went through almost revolutionary changes during the war years. Pre-1914, women had been seen as wilting beauties, impeded by boned corsets and rarely used to work more strenuous than a gentle game of croquet or a piano duet. A decade later, women had cut their hair, raised their hemlines and smoked like chimneys. They had earned the right to do so by doing their bit. How shocked their grandmothers would have been.

Back to Blighty

Soldiers on Leave

For the British Tommy, leave was a rare luxury, granted on average every 14 months. There was usually little forewarning and most soldiers arrived at their own front door dirty, louse-ridden and exhausted. Time allocated was seven days, although for those who lived several hundred miles from London, a few additional days would be granted to account for extra travelling.

In 1915, *The Graphic* published a picture of an officer enjoying the rarefied environs of a first class train carriage on his way to Boulogne. The accompanying editorial explained:

> *The worries of war are soon forgotten by our young officers when they get leave to spend a few days at home. A sleepy railway journey in France, a rapid crossing of the Channel (with no fear of German submarines) and the peace of England is theirs. Then a round of visits, the delights of town, perhaps a little shooting, and then back to the trenches or wherever duty calls in Flanders or France. It is a pleasant and nerve-soothing interlude.*

It was probably only a privileged fraction of the army who enjoyed 'a little shooting' while on leave, but for most soldiers, whether officer or private, the long-anticipated time away from the Front was an experience met with ambivalence. Some would savour the luxury of home comforts, but also feel some level of disconnection from their former lives.

This confusing emotional conflict and sense of alienation stemmed from a number of factors. Men felt a deep bond with men in their unit, and such intense comradeship, like an invisible umbilical cord, reeled men back with a mix of loyalty and obligation. While at home, it was almost impossible for a man to disassociate himself from what was happening at the Front, and for those who returned to find familiar faces no longer there, this confusion

The Horrors of Peace', Edwin Morrow, *The Bystander*, 20 January 1915
Caption: *From the dangerous, but dreary routine of life in the trenches Tommy returns home to recuperate at his ease, only to find that Peace hath her horrors 'no less renowned than War'.*
Three wounded soldiers enjoy the dubious thrill of a ride in a motor car driven by a lady chauffeur with a need for speed, and probably wonder if it might have been safer to remain in the trenches! The background scenery in Edwin Morrow's picture is appropriately patriotic, from the miniature flag waved by a small child to the Union Jack coat on the flagpole in the background.

was compounded by feelings of guilt and responsibility, as if their presence might have somehow saved others. Bruce Bairnsfather found life in the trenches shocking, but his personal coping mechanism was to regularly decline leave, for fear he would be unable to return. In his own words:

> It's a curious feeling, this wanting to go back. Nobody could possibly want to go back to life in the trenches or to participate in an offensive...But it's because all your pals are out there at the front, and all the people who really matter are at the front; that's why you long to be one of them, and in with them, in the big job in hand.

Those in front-line service shared an unspoken, complicit understanding, a common experience impossible to articulate to those enjoying what seemed like comparative safety in England. A soldier's personal exposure to squalor, suffering and death was a burden that simply could not be shared with family and friends, even if social conventions had allowed for such candour. Many just did not wish to upset those close to them by revealing the truth. To some extent, this disengagement with 'normal' society led to resentment in varying degrees and to a polarising gulf of understanding between the men at the Front and the civilians at home. Edmund Blunden, writing in *Undertones of War*, commented on the

> large decay of lively bright love of country, the crystallisation of dull, civilian hatred on the basis of 'the last drop of blood', and the fact that the German air raids had persuaded my London friends that London was the sole battlefront.

Soldiers at the Front felt they walked in the shadow of death daily, and to witness the home front's preoccupation with bombing raids, or complaints about relatively minor irritations such as rationing or even the shortage of servants, filled some of those on leave with disgust. Sudden exposure to rich food and a society that carried on despite the conflict raging just a few hundred miles from their ballrooms, as well as the sight of some young men not in uniform, all underpinned this sense of injustice and maladjustment.

On the whole, magazine illustrators sympathised with the plight of the homecoming soldier. They ridiculed interfering and ignorant do-gooders who demanded details from wounded soldiers. Nationwide pessimism and gloomy headlines were portrayed as an ungrateful attitude to show when men were risking life and limb to defend the Empire, while hosts requesting the pleasure of the company of soldiers on leave are depicted as demanding and insensitive.

Other scenes, however, show the positive side to coming home on leave. The tranquillity and satisfaction of seeing one's family, the admiration and support given by strangers to anyone in khaki or the glorious joy of a soft, clean bed were all pleasures heightened by the awful conditions experienced at the Front. For soldiers who were returning to England to recover from wounds, the relief must have been immense. Getting a 'Blighty', a wound serious enough to require passage on the first departing hospital ship, was a means of honourable escape, and it meant that recuperation could be aided by friends and families. As men recovered, however, they were monitored to assess their fitness, and if recovery was rapid and fitness acceptable, they were likely to return to France.

The bittersweet nature of leave of any kind meant that the most difficult aspect was having to part from loved ones at the end of it. One soldier refused leave, telling his Commanding Officer, 'I said Goodbye, Sir when we left home. I couldn't stand it again.'

Personal application is first made to the Orderly Corporal, giving Age, Number, Height, Religion, Previous Convictions, etc., etc., etc.

When pass is due you ask the Orderly Sergeant, who refers you to—

The Company-Sergeant-Major, who sends you to—

The Battalion-Sergeant-Major, who directs you to—

Your Company Officer who sends you back to—

The Orderly Sergeant, who had it all the time, but can't bear parting with it

"You are then just in time—for this!"

The Illustrated London News Christmas Number front cover, unattributed artist,
The Illustrated London News, 1915

While magazines like *The Tatler* and *The Sketch* flaunted modern, graphic images on their Christmas covers, the more traditional *ILN* remained loyal to the sentimental Victorian-style narrative, which drew on themes of heroism and family values. Here, a homecoming soldier, an older man and a husband and father, is greeted by his three children as their mother points out the focal point of the painting – a Victoria Cross medal attached to his chest.

'Week-End Leave and How to Obtain It – An experience that has been, and is being, regularly endured by many thousands of our readers', J. H. Thorpe, *The Bystander*, 8 December 1915

For any 21st-century British worker who feels short-changed by their 25-day quota of annual leave, spare a thought for British soldiers during World War I, who were lucky to get one week every 14 months from what was arguably the worst job imaginable. This poor private works his way up through a bureaucratic chain of command only to find that he misses his train. He is likely to have being heading for the nearest town, or better still, Paris, where theatres and cafés continued to thrive and were a magnetic draw to soldiers on leave.

'Keeping the Home Fires Burning', Fred Buchanan, *The Bystander*, 9 February 1916

Caption: *The Man from the Trenches (to the Man from the North Sea): 'What a bloomin' cheerful country to lie awake at night for!'*

The enthusiasm that had whipped the country into a patriotic fervour in 1914 began slowly to pall as the war progressed, and news of defeats and the troubled Gallipoli campaign dominated the press.

Soldiers at the Front felt that this blanket reporting did little to recognise the impossible conditions, the ceaseless stalemate of trench warfare, and the almost daily displays of courage. These two men probably feel that if anybody should be glum and disillusioned, it should be them. Both show a trademark cheery optimism, a commonly projected and accepted characteristic of the British soldier promulgated by illustrators.

Above: 'Ex Pede Herculem', Bert Thomas, *The Bystander*, 5 January 1916

Caption: *Urchin (to Mick — just back from the trenches): 'Shine, sir?'*

Mick: 'Away wid ye; would yez deproive me of me bit o' glory'

Right: 'Experience', Frank Reynolds, *The Sketch*, 16 February 1916

Caption: *The Small Boy (to his father — just returned from the trenches): 'I say, you'll cop it when muvver sees your boots!'*

Most privates lived and slept in the clothes on their back, and they would return home with the mud of Flanders still encrusted on their uniform. As Bert Thomas's Irish soldier knows, dirty boots were a badge of honour, although one wonders how welcome those boots might have been in a house-proud wife's kitchen. Bert Thomas (1883–1966), one of the great 'black and white men', produced one of the war's most popular images, ''Arf a mo' Kaiser', showing a cheeky Tommy pausing to light a cigarette. Thomas drew the picture in ten minutes for the 'Smokes for Tommy' campaign, run by the *Weekly Dispatch*. Its popularity raised a quarter of a million pounds to be used to buy tobacco for men at the front. Thomas was a regular contributor to *Punch* as well as to *The Sketch* and *The Bystander*. A chain-smoker himself, the ubiquitous cigarette can be seen stuck to the lips of his Irish soldier.

'Blighty, Sweet Blighty!', Will Owen, *The Sketch*, 5 July 1916

Caption: *Tommy (home on leave after fifteen months in the trenches and ready to praise all familiar things): 'Hey Jimmy! Don't the gas-works smell lovely!'*

How alien England must have seemed after more than a year in the trenches. These two Tommies are determined to see (or smell) the good in everything as they stick their heads out of a crowded train. The smell of the Front, perfumed with the scent of decaying bodies, scorched earth and open latrines, could be unbearable and the gas-works of home were probably a vast improvement.

'The Horrors of Home', Arthur Watts, *The Bystander*, 19 June 1918

Caption: *Captain Jones, being on leave, runs down to his old home at Long-Puddle Minor for a few days' peace and quiet deep in the countryside*

It may be an exaggeration to suggest that small rural backwaters were routinely transformed into belching hearts of industry during World War I, but this Arthur Watts picture does highlight the massive channelling of civilian effort into an industry whose sole purpose was to feed the Front with shells.

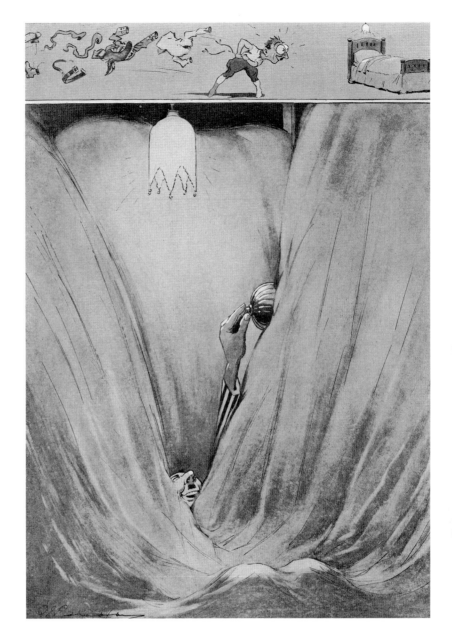

Above: 'Home From the Trenches – How Tommy Got To Sleep', J. H. Dowd,
The Illustrated Sporting and Dramatic News, 30 January 1915
Right: 'Joys of To-Day V – The Delightfulness of the common or feather bed to the
man on leave', George Studdy, *The Sketch*, 19 December 1917
While on front-line duty, soldiers would be required to sleep where they could – usually
in any hollow or funk hole along the trench wall, although some of the more comfortable
dug-outs might have small beds. For battalions travelling up, or spending time behind the
lines, sleep might be in the open air, a cow byre or an abandoned church. Tiredness
was all-consuming, but of course, considering the circumstances, sleep was fitful.
Unsurprisingly, the prospect of a good night's sleep was one of the simple joys of being
home. George Studdy's soldier sinks into joyful, downy ecstasy, while J. H. Dowd's picture
highlights the struggle many men had to endure to shake off the habits and routine of
trench life. (Above: © George Studdy/ILN Picture Library)

'Blighted "Blighty" – The Sad Sufferings of a Subaltern on Leave', Reginald Cleaver, *The Bystander*, 22 August 1917

A rather skewed sense of priority here finds a bemused junior officer discovering that his war-obsessed friends and family have plunged wholeheartedly into supporting the war effort, much to his incredulous dismay. A parade of committee members, fundraisers, nurses, FANYs and Land Girls all put their duties before him. Considering the casualty figures, you would think they could make an exception in his case.

'War-Time Studdys! III – Frightfulness as applied to the man on short leave', George Studdy, *The Sketch*, 19 April 1916

For many men returning home on leave, their main priority was to rest and savour the peace and quiet of home. George Studdy's poor soldier finds it is not always so easy with the obligation of unwanted social invitations ever present. (© George Studdy/ILN Picture Library)

'The Latest Mode de la Guerre in the rue de la Paix – Khaki-clad London Buyers "inspecting" Mannequines', L. Sabattier, *The Sketch*, 3 March 1915

Many artists whose work appeared in illustrated magazines managed to combine military service with their chosen trade through the war. They weren't the only ones. Here, two British officers temporarily revert to their civilian careers as fashion buyers at a London department store and view the latest 'modes' at a Parisian salon. *The Sketch* ran weekly fashion pages so this picture, placing soldiers in such an incongruous setting, would have been of special interest to its readers. Sabattier, another of the main artists at *L'Illustration* magazine, mainly illustrated scenes from behind the lines, and had a particular fondness for drawing pictures of pretty nurses, many of which were reproduced in *The Illustrated War News*.

'A Soldier's Homecoming from the Battlefields of France', J. Simont, *The Sphere*, 26 January 1918

This carefully constructed painting by J. Simont shows a scene almost photographic in its realism. It is as if you can hear the hum of Gallic conversation and smell the French polish on the table as three sons return home on leave to wives, sisters, mothers, children and sweethearts. Simont was the principal artist for *L'Illustration* (a French equivalent to *The Illustrated London News* or *The Sphere*) for 20 years and in terms of style and subject there are parallels with Fortunino Matania. Both artists' work was reproduced in illustrated magazines in Allied countries and in those of the Central Powers.

Above: 'War Types to-Date – No.3 – The Lady Who Wants to Know How He Got It!',
Sub-Lieutenant Arthur Watts RNVR, *The Bystander*, **27 October 1915**
Right: 'The Incorrigible Altruist', Ralph Cleaver, *The Bystander*, **26 April 1916**
Caption: *Old Lady: 'And how did you get wounded, my poor fellow?'*
The Hero: 'By not minding my own business, and interfering in this bloomin' war!'
(Note to the Attorney-General – This is not intended to suggest a mutinous attitude on the part of the British soldier,
only his sarcastic habit of speech – ED.)

Most soldiers returned to their former lives with the haunting images and memories of the Front firmly locked away deep inside. Civilians were largely ignorant of the psychological scars behind the physical ones; an oversight not entirely their fault, as the truly ghastly details of war were rarely discussed. Pats on the back and a free beer in the pub might be the advantages of coming home on leave, but equally, curiosity and interference on the part of well-wishers was not always welcome. Both of these pictures mock the familiar character of the altruistic do-gooder, preying on wounded soldiers. Note the caveat inserted by the editor at the end of Cleaver's picture, anxious to allay any doubts about the magazine's patriotic allegiance.

'The Trophy', Edmund Blampied, *The Sphere*, 29 November 1915

The trophy in question is a German Pickelhaube helmet, displayed with pride by a recuperating soldier. He lies in an immaculate bed in the company of an elegantly dressed lady and her fashionable Pomeranian dog. Of course, it is a stylish and sanitised view of a wounded soldier, a suitably innocuous scene for the front cover of *The Sphere*'s Christmas number. Many soldiers returned home with injuries that were disfiguring, and 250,000 British soldiers lost limbs during the World War I. (© Estate of Edmund Blampied/ILN Picture Library)

'Well, Goodbye, Nurse!', Christopher Clark, *The Sphere*, 29 November 1915

Nurses retained an almost hallowed status, exuding a calm serenity and religious purity. This vision in white in a hospital in Blighty must have been an arresting sight after months living among shades of muddy brown. For women who donned the nurse's uniform, it afforded them a respect not always granted to other women's volunteer services – a respect that shines through in this picture.

Shoulder to Shoulder

Allies

From its earliest issues, *The Illustrated London News* considered itself a publication with a truly global perspective. This inherent cosmopolitanism ensured it would always pay generous attention to the appearance, characteristics, idiosyncrasies and exploits of Britain's allies and by doing so, answer the natural inquisitiveness of its readers.

From the gritty determination of Piou-Piou to the muscular confidence of the US doughboys, Britain's allies, along with troops from around the Empire and British dominions, transformed the Western Front into a global melting pot. *The Illustrated London News* and *The Graphic* assigned 'special artists' to the different seats of war to send back an impression of Britain's allies for the public at home. John Wladimiroff for *The Graphic* spent time with the Russian forces, while Seppings Wright did the same for the *ILN*. Frederic Villiers, in his sixties and approaching the end of a distinguished career, visited the French trenches on several occasions, as did Paul Thiriat for *The Sphere*. Bairnsfather not only caricatured the British and American troops, but was invited to do the same to the French and the Italians. Helen McKie, unusually for a woman, travelled extensively around Europe during this period, and was in Poland just before war broke out, promptly sending back sketches of Britain's Russian comrades.

Serving soldiers such as Bairnsfather or Lawson Wood could draw from their own experience to provide occasionally accurate, though often stereotypical, depictions of foreign soldiers. Meanwhile, civilian artists back at home used eyewitness accounts, photographs and a sprinkling of imagination to come up with their own interpretations.

'The Whip Hand', Bruce Bairnsfather, *The Bystander*, 11 October 1916

Caption: *Private Mulligatawny (the Australian stock-whip wonder) frequently causes a lot of bother in the enemy's trenches*

Bruce Bairnsfather's 'stock-whip' cartoon sums up the practical, self-reliant, rough and ready boldness associated with the Aussies. Most Anzac troops were deployed in the Middle East, and of course at Gallipoli, before being sent to the Western Front in 1916 (the time of this picture). The Australians were no walkover, and many felt bitterly let down by what they considered the badly judged British command and the resultant poorly organised British troops. One Australian mining engineer railed against the 'British staff, British methods and British bungling'. The Australians and the New Zealanders proportionately suffered some of the highest losses of the war, and the image of the Anzac soldier remains one of the most iconic.

The French, who fought in their hundreds of thousands along the Western Front, holding different sectors from the British, were the most frequently illustrated. French civilians in particular played an important role in the average British Tommy's experience of being abroad for the first time. Many provided billet accommodation for soldiers; others, some typical Gallic hospitality in local bars or *estaminets* where wine and *pommes frites* – and the accommodating girls – were a welcome diversion from trench life. For those who missed their wives and children, it could be a great comfort to have contact with French families, injecting some normality into what were unusually abnormal circumstances.

The British press had a particular sympathy for Belgium, and despite its moniker of 'brave, little Belgium' and the numerous reports and pictures of refugees, the small Belgian army's valiant stand against the Germans had been impressive, appealing to the British love of the underdog. The Belgians' pluck was embodied by their royal family. After the German invasion, King Albert moved his government to Le Havre and continued to command his troops, despite the wishes of the French and British commanders. His eldest boy, the Duke of Brabant, attended Eton alongside Prince Henry, and fuzzy-haired Princess Marie-Jose was the darling of the British press.

Three New Army divisions made up of 210,000 men were raised in Ireland. The 36th (Ulster) Division, comprising mainly Protestant Unionists, contained a substantial proportion of men from the Ulster Volunteer Force, while the 10th (Irish) and 16th (Irish) Divisions were formed from Nationalist, mainly Catholic Irishmen. It was a politically sensitive time for Ireland, which was on the verge of rebellion, but both Unionists and Nationalists hoped a swift British victory would refocus Britain's attention on the Home Rule issue, and put aside their differences to fight for a common cause.

Of course, soldiers from further corners of the Empire fought, and often died, thousands of miles from home. The Meerut and Lahore divisions (Indian Army) were fascinating for their exoticism, and tolerated treacherous, alien conditions to exhibit great bravery and resilience at the battle of Neuve Chapelle in March 1915 and the Second Battle of Ypres in April 1915.

Overall, the number of the Empire's dead makes sobering reading. Out of almost 620,000 Canadian troops, 60,000 were killed and a further 150,000 wounded. Out of 300,000 Australian men who went to Europe, there were 180,000 casualties and of 90,000 New Zealanders, 47,000 were casualties. The Indian army sent nearly 160,000 men to France and 25,000 were killed or wounded.

The Australians and New Zealanders held a particular romantic fascination. In *The Anzac Book*, an annual edited by the journalist Charles Bean, the archetypal Australian bushman – independent, proficient and physically resilient – was idealised into the Anzac myth. Many of their 'Pommie' allies regarded them as feral mavericks; but, reared in the Australian outback or the rugged mountains of New Zealand, their rough and tough image in many ways perfectly suited them to the conditions of the Western Front. The Anzacs' vociferous criticism of the British command after Gallipoli and Pozieres in 1916 sealed their reputation for having an egalitarian disregard for traditional rank and status. One Tasmanian grazier cursed the British officers at Fromelles as 'Pommie Jackeroos and just as hopeless…most of them crawlers or favourites of some toff.' Despite their criticisms of the British, the Australians usually exempted Scottish units, who exemplified their own hardy bravery.

Of course it was the arrival of the Americans that provoked the greatest wave of excitement and indeed, America's entry into the war proved a decisive turning point. But they had taken their time and the prevaricating neutrality of Uncle Sam was the subject of countless satirical cartoons. As with each nation that fought in the war, the Americans had a range of physical characteristics and mannerisms that artists were quick to plunder. In their eyes, the Americans were well-built, laid-back, craggy-jawed and spoke with that exotically confident drawl. Bruce Bairnsfather was asked to spend time with the American forces to produce some morale-boosting cartoons and immediately warmed to the doughboys, though he was astonished by their capacity for food, describing a plateful of 12 fried eggs destined for just one man.

The men of various nationalities who fought in World War I had been thrust upon each other by international treaties and circumstances beyond their control, yet, though intrinsically alien to one another, they were obliged to bond together to achieve a common aim. Within the population, both civilian and combatant, there was engendered a certain degree of cultural discovery and tolerance, albeit one created out of artificial conditions. It is a strange irony that even the smallest amount of racial harmony should be born out of a global conflict.

'The Allies Shoulder to Shoulder at Ypres', Balliol Salmon, *The Graphic*, 30 January 1915

Pictures like this, showing French infantry charging alongside Irish Guards and Grenadiers at Ypres, project a strong message of camaraderie among the Allies. It was drawn from a description by Private P. Gilleece of the Irish Guards, who lost his left arm and three fingers in the action, 'cut clean off by pieces of shrapnel'. Balliol Salmon, who worked for *The Graphic*, *The Illustrated London News* and *The Illustrated Sporting and Dramatic News* was, according to Percy Bradshaw of The Press Art School, more at home drawing the 'pretty girl and handsome man' picture. He was one of the few artists able to work in Russian charcoal (which was useless in perspiring hands) and soon specialised in another popular creation, 'the young lady of fifteen', as illustrator of the well-known Angela Brazil books.

'Refuge', S. Eduardo, *The Sphere*, 5 January 1918

A picture that shows civilians can be casualties of war as much as combatants was painted by Eduardo Matania, father of Fortunino (who signed himself 'S. Eduardo'). The mother and her four children, who find shelter from an unseen battle outside, have obviously only had to time to hastily pack a few essentials and the absence of a father, probably fighting at the Front, makes the picture all the more poignant. It was published in 1918, at a time when the Germans were making further advances into France, resulting in a new wave of refugees reminiscent of the 1914 flight.

'"Tommy Atkins" quite at home in France: British soldiers making friends with French children and receiving country refreshments', Frederic de Haenen, *The Illustrated War News*, 26 August 1914
The enthusiasm and warmth shown by the French towards the British Expeditionary Force in the first few weeks of the war was, according to reports in magazines, quite overwhelming. This charming drawing by Frederic de Haenen shows a group of Tommies enjoying some Gallic hospitality; food and drink are generously offered while small French children have immediately made friends.

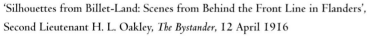

'Silhouettes from Billet-Land: Scenes from Behind the Front Line in Flanders',
Second Lieutenant H. L. Oakley, *The Bystander,* **12 April 1916**
With just a pair of scissors, H. L. Oakley conveys the pleasures of staying in a French billet
'after a turn in the trenches'. He adds: 'The officers usually occupy rooms in the farmhouse,
while the soldiers make themselves as comfortable as they can in the huge barns that are part
of every French farm. Anything is preferable to the trenches, and even if his sleeping quarters
are sometimes shared with cows or goats, Tommy soon makes himself at home.'

'Piou-Piou Junior', Helen McKie, *The Bystander,* 13 January 1915
This picture by Helen McKie (who would continue to send drawings from Paris and the
French Riviera in the glamorous 1920s and 30s) shows a group of French conscripts going
to report themselves at headquarters, 'at least as cheerfully to the service of his country as the
"volunteer" Briton' , and the caption adds, hinting heavily, 'in much larger numbers'. French
private soldiers were known as 'Piou-Piou', or 'Poilou', the equivalent of the British 'Tommy'.
Poilou translates as 'hairy' or 'virile'!

'After 100 years – "Pass, Friends. All's Well". 1815, Waterloo. 1915, ! Berlin',
Lawson Wood, *The Illustrated Sporting and Dramatic News,* **2 January 1915**

There was a certain irony in the fact that a century before, France and Britain had faced each other across the battlefield of Waterloo. Once described as 'natural and necessary enemies', by the 18th-century British ambassador, the Earl of Stair, King Edward VII had done much to foster relations between the two countries, diplomacy that bore fruit in the Entente Cordiale agreement of 1904. The agreement formed an official bond of friendship between the countries and resolved long-standing disputes over territories and trade routes in North Africa, Canada and the Far East. (© Estate of Lawson Wood/ILN Picture Library)

'The Judgement of Paris', George Studdy, *The Illustrated Sporting and Dramatic News,*
17 April 1915

The kilted Highland regiments were the subject of fascination among the French, who were unused to the novelty of men in skirts. In George Studdy's picture (where this time, the girl does the choosing), reports about the irresistibility of the tartan must mean that the favour would be bestowed upon the soldier in the kilt. Charles Inman Barnard described troops arriving in Boulogne in August 1914: 'The prettiest girls in every town throw flowers and kisses to these stalwart British lads…Highland regiments wearing the kilt have stupendous success with the blushing young women of France', while Helen McKie in *The Graphic* describes 'one highland soldier in a street in Paris. He was followed by an admiring little crowd, and people of all classes stopped to shake hands with him, much to his good-natured embarrassment.' (© George Studdy/ILN Picture Library)

'1914 – Pat-Riots, 1915 – Patriots', Alick P. F. Ritchie, *The Bystander*,
24 March 1915

In July 1914, following decades of unrest over British dominion, Ireland was on the verge of civil war. Its future relied on the establishment of Home Rule legislation but the outbreak of war halted progress abruptly. 210,000 Irishmen, both Nationalist and Unionist, swelled the British effort on the Western Front. Some believed that aiding the British would eventually help them attain their political ends, although many joined up for the usual mix of reasons given by any other British Tommy. Alick P. F. Ritchie's before and after cartoon, which suggests a stereotypical view of the factious Irish turned into 'reformed', true patriots by joining up, fails to recognise, like so many, that the Irish question was not going to disappear.

'Allies: Gallant Russia', Archibald Wells, *The Sketch*, 9 December 1914

Part of a series of designs by Archibald Wells, this Russian soldier sports the beard so closely identified with his race. He also wears a heavy greatcoat and shiny boots and looks rather debonair. The Russian uniform consisted of a *ghymnasterka* (gymnastic) blouse and an olive green loose tunic first adopted during the Russo-Japanese War. Like most Russian Cossacks he wears an *astrakhan* hat. Perhaps the accompanying girl represents the Ballets Russe which had caused such a stir in London in 1912.

'Allies: Brave Belgium', Archibald Wells, *The Sketch*, 9 December 1914

This companion picture to 'Gallant Russia' shows a Belgian cavalryman against the backdrop of the combined Union Jack and Belgian flags, a symbol of the two countries' entwined loyalties. Britain initially entered the war to defend Belgium against the German breach of a treaty dating back to 1839, which had guaranteed Belgian neutrality. This neutrality meant that, although Belgium had maintained an army, it was no match for one the size of Germany. The British press championed the Belgians but played particularly on the quainter aspects of its army, publishing, for example, many pictures of the guns traditionally drawn by dogs. The Belgians made a valiant stand against the invading Germans, but were eventually driven to the far west of their country.

Above: 'A Black Outlook', Will Owen, *The Bystander*, 25 November 1914
Right: 'East and West', Sydney Adamson, *The Illustrated Sporting and Dramatic News*,
22 May 1915

The title of Will Owen's picture, showing two Sikh soldiers with bayonets fixed, waiting to ambush a smug German on horseback, belongs to another era, but despite the pun on ethnicity, the British greatly respected the two Indian infantry and one cavalry divisions that fought on the Western Front in 1915. Racial stereotyping is put aside in Sydney Adamson's picture, drawn from a description by an officer present at Neuve Chapelle, recalling a scene in which an Indian soldier stops to comfort a dying Highlander in the midst of battle. 'He gave him water, "to ease the passing of his soul," as Kipling puts it, and the Highlander died in his arms'. World War I is often assumed to be a white man's war, and certainly the main protagonists were white Europeans. Yet, as well as Indian and Gurkha regiments, there were many African units in the French army, plus the British West Indian Regiment recruited from Jamaica and Barbados. Racial tension certainly existed, but interaction and communication, induced by a shared common experience, improved during the course of the war. African American troops also fought, but were strictly segregated from the white Americans. Two divisions instead fought with the French.

'Great Scot! Some Growth!', Wilmot Lunt, *The Bystander* front cover, 16 October 1918

Canada's contribution to the war was massive, as the caption from this picture of October 1918 confirms: 'At the beginning of last month, it had sent 390,000 soldiers overseas and 60,000 were in training.' But according to a *Times* report from October 1914, this gigantic Canadian is more than representative of numerical force. *The Times* reporter was obviously much impressed by the physical appearance of the Canadians arriving at Plymouth: 'Their height and girth are remarkably good. They are the type of strong, clean-limbed Briton at whom one instinctively takes a second look in the street.' Such admiration makes the loss of 130,000 of these young, wholesome and handsome Canadians all the more poignant.

'India's First-Class Fighting Men in Action: A Ghurkha Charge Which the Germans Could Not Face', J. Dodworth, *The Graphic*, 5 December 1914

The Gurkhas, one of Britain's oldest allies, have always had a reputation for outstanding bravery and their performance in World War I was no exception. Two of their number won the VC and the Gurkhas were the only Allied troops to take the crest of Hill Q at Gallipoli on 6 August 1915 (though forced back due to a mistaken Allied bombardment). In this instance, German troops decide to turn and flee, rather than face the formidable charging Gurkhas.

'A Visit to the Alpini: 19**?', Bruce Bairnsfather, *The Bystander*, 27 March 1918

Caption: *The war was over some time ago, but this man hasn't heard about it yet, and nobody can get up to tell him. His sniping is therefore very annoying to that Austrian village in the valley.*

Charles Dana Gibson, the great American illustrator and founder of *Life* magazine, was Head of the American Division of Pictorial Publicity during World War I. He considered this cartoon to be 'the most brilliant thing Bairnsfather ever did'. The Italian army specifically asked Bairnsfather to visit the Italian Front in 1917, where, in the company of the Duke of Milan, he endured white-knuckle car rides around hairpin bends, followed by treks on mules to get to the Front. Bairnsfather greatly admired the Alpini. All the mountain troops, including the Austrian Landesschutzen and the Bavarian Alpenkorps, were regarded as elite within their individual armies.

'A Swiss Shepherd Watching a Battle by the Frontier', W. Heath Robinson, *The Illustrated Sporting and Dramatic News*, 16 January 1915

In many ways, nothing sums up the absurdity of war better than this picture by Heath Robinson, whose Swiss shepherd sits serenely enjoying his pipe amidst tranquil, bucolic surroundings, while calmly observing the military melée in progress two metres over the border. Switzerland's democratic, federal constitution was formed in 1848, and, determined to retain its neutral status, it refused to join any military alliances. Nevertheless, contrary to Heath Robinson's vision, the war did mean Switzerland was forced to conscript men to defend her borders and sharpened existing frictions between French and German speakers within the cantons. (© Mrs J. C. Robinson by kind permission of the proprietor and Pollinger Limited/ILN Picture Library)

'The Neutral Umbrella', W. Edward Wigfall, *The Bystander*, 12 April 1916

Caption: *The Trio: 'It doesn't seem to be much protection, does it?'*

Holland, Norway and the USA find that a small umbrella of neutrality offers little metaphorical protection from the ravages of war. All three countries had been affected by German submarine warfare. British blockades of Germany cut off a vital trading link for Norway, who then suffered substantial losses at sea at the hands of German U-boats (about half of her merchant fleet). Holland found her usual commercial routes to the Dutch East Indies blocked and was inundated with Belgian refugees at a cost of 37 million guilders.

'America's Contribution in Men to the Allied Forces', S. Ugo, *The Sphere*, 1 February 1919

This rousing picture by Ugo Matania (who signed his work 'S. Ugo'), reminiscent of Montgomery Flagg's famous US recruiting poster, represents the American contribution to the war. In 1914 the US regular army was extremely small, just 100,000, but public opinion and an energetic recruitment drive meant that, by 2 July 1918, it was officially announced that 1,019,000 had sailed for Europe.

Above: 'America to Germany: "If you don't darned well stop this submarine business, and cease your murderous attacks on American citizens we'll-er-er, we'll-hum-er-well-we'll jolly well send you another firm Note"', Thomas Maybank, *The Bystander* front cover, 21 July 1915

Right: 'Can He Stay There?', Alfred Leete, *The Bystander* front cover, 24 February 1915
After the torpedoing of the Cunard passenger liner, *Lusitania*, in May 1915, Britain felt sure the United States would enter the war. She did, but not until two years after the event, leading to much satirising of Uncle Sam's hesitation and rather ineffective attempts at diplomacy. In fact, Woodrow Wilson won a second term of presidency in 1916 with the slogan, 'He kept us out of the war', although Germany's continuing submarine warfare eventually led to his capitulation. Alfred Leete's cartoon sums up the precarious balancing act required for America's isolationist policy. Even when America did join it was as an 'associate power' rather than as a member of the Allies.

'The Restraining Hand', E. T. Reed, *The Bystander*, 27 October 1915

Depicted by E. T. Reed as a ditherer in thrall to the Kaiser, Constantine I, King of the Hellenes, was in an unenviable position when war broke out. His wife, Queen Sophie, was a younger sister of the Kaiser, and he himself had had German military training. Constantine knew his country had far more to lose by joining the Triple Entente than by remaining neutral, but the King's first minister, Eleftherios Venizelos, supported the Allies and formed a separate government, raising an army of 20,000 to fight the Bulgarians in Macedonia. After the French navy began a siege of Athens, Constantine had no choice but to abdicate. His son Alexander promised to work with Venizelos and by July 1918, 250,000 Greeks were fighting in Macedonia.

'"Lusitania!" "Lusitania!": The Americans' Battle Cry', Fortunino Matania, *The Sphere*, 20 July 1918

The Americans had to wait a long time to avenge the *Lusitania*. An Australian officer observed, 'It is a curious fact that, with less provocation than the French, who see their own towns destroyed before their eyes and a great belt of ruin across their country, a world of tragedy where their own families are separated from them by the German lines, the American soldiers have come over here with such stern spirit and with no kind of forgiveness in their hearts for the men who have caused all this misery.'

'London as Cosmopolis: Uniforms of all Allies in one Restaurant Lounge', Helen McKie, *The Bystander*, 26 April 1916

Helen McKie's bustling London restaurant is a sophisticated mix of glamorous British society and a truly international blend of dashing men in uniform, a sight that would have turned heads a decade before but that now barely raises an eyebrow. Other than Paris, London, where restaurants and theatres continued to thrive, was the other obvious destination for the more well-heeled Allied officers.

'He Soon Found It', Bruce Bairnsfather, *The Bystander*, 1 May 1918

In June 1918, during the German offensive that pushed the line to 56 miles from Paris, retreating French troops advised an American Marine officer to fall back, to which Captain Lloyd Williams famously replied, 'Retreat? Hell, we only just got here.' This gutsy, no-nonsense wise-cracking is personified by Bairnsfather's US officer advising a new arrival to keep walking straight until he gets to the fighting. Bairnsfather was 'hired' early in 1918 by the US Army which hoped he would do for them what he had done for the British. He had enormous success and would later make several lecture tours around the States.

Venus & Mars

Love & Marriage in Wartime

Before 1914, illustrators could always rely on the subject of romance to offer them humorous and aesthetic inspiration. Some, like William Barribal or the American Charles Dana Gibson (whose voluptuous Gibson Girls were published in Britain by *The Illustrated London News* in the 1890s), made their name by painting beautiful girls replete with seductive promise. Others, such as Harold Earnshaw, perhaps more empathetic to the obstacles faced by the average courting couple in 1913, tended to draw awkward exchanges between gauche lovers.

War inevitably and immediately placed the population in a heightened and sharpened emotional state, a fact not lost on illustrators who found that both the physical and intangible trappings of war – uniforms, love letters, heroism and separation – added to a theme already rich in possibilities. What better way to appeal to a readership who increasingly wished to be reminded of the good things in life than by painting love, the antithesis of war? In a less cynical age, the motif of the brave husband or sweetheart taking leave of a doe-eyed girl to march off to serve King and Country was a powerful one, and artists were as quick to exploit it as publishers were to print it. While the *ILN* and *The Sphere* remained focused on illustration charting the progress of the war and of its events and battles, *The Sketch*, *The Tatler* and *The Bystander*, all of which had a fun and frivolous reputation, continued to commission and print illustrations on the broad theme of love – at an even greater rate than before the war. So it was that romance remained a staple of the artist's repertoire.

Romantic pictures, even humorous ones, reflected a universal emotion affecting those left behind as intensely as their loved ones fighting abroad. A young bride left at home might not ever comprehend the horrors of trench warfare, but she could identify with the yearning loneliness and desire experienced by men at the Front. Illustrations that could communicate a

'A False Alarm', Wilmot Lunt, *The Illustrated Sporting and Dramatic News* **Christmas Number, 'Holly Leaves', December 1917**
World War I was a watershed in many ways, not least in the gradual breaking down of established courtship rituals and sexual conventions. A quality periodical would touch only lightly on the reality of actual physical relationships, and the innocence of Wilmot Lunt's picture suggests little more than a couple disturbed by the family dog during a kiss. Nevertheless, upper-class girls of the previous generation would rarely have been left alone with any man, let alone a suitor.

shared sense of longing naturally struck a chord, as did those representing the subtly changing attitudes to sex and relationships – another social by-product of the Great War. Fred Pegram's series of illustrations for Kenilworth cigarettes are a fine example, showing couples in moments of shared intimacy that might have been unthinkable before the war. It is also notable that *The Sketch* exclusively published the work of Raphael Kirchner, the first 'pin-up' artist, whose paintings catered to lonely soldiers looking for something a little more (acceptably) risqué.

Some romantically themed pictures often reveal a rather cunning sub-plot. Many deal with idolatry, depicting any man in uniform as the object of female admiration and adoration. Others depict soldiers home on leave enjoying fragrant company and feminine attention. The message is clear: join up, lads, and the girls will come running. It seems a rather naïve propagandist ploy to modern eyes, but it was certainly more subtle than many other recruitment techniques.

As the war progressed and casualty lists grew, the ratio of men and women of marriageable age became seriously imbalanced, and in Britain, the male species became an increasingly rare breed. A soldier back in Blighty became as much a subject of fascination as did a woman in the male environment of the Front. The tiresome aspects of female attention were treated with customary wry humour by many illustrators, who delighted in showing nervous VC winners about to be introduced to rooms overflowing with enthusiastic female admirers, or men in uniform being worshipped by crowds of wistful schoolgirls. But it is a humour with a bitterly poignant reality; many women of that generation never found a husband. By 1918, despite demobilisation leading to a temporary upsurge in marriages, there simply were not enough men to go round.

Nevertheless, the subject of weddings – increasingly fleeting occasions – was a regular theme. The period of 1915–16 did see a sharp rise in the marriage rate (19.4 per thousand, compared to pre-war levels of 15 per thousand), perhaps in part due to the fact that until mid-1916 military recruitment was still centred on an unmarried male population. A more likely explanation is that as the war dragged on, a 'live for the day' mentality saw men and women choosing to tie the knot before it was too late, sometimes (for those who married while on leave) with the clock quite literally ticking.

Separation from loved ones brought its own worries. Trust diluted and jealousy inflamed, lovers' anxieties were given a comic magnitude by illustrators, but perhaps not without some basis of truth. A subaltern recuperating in a field hospital might wonder who was making overtures to his eligible fiancée back at home, while she might well be suspicious of the nurse written of so eloquently in his letters.

Love, of course, had its tragic side. Despite the light-heartedness of most of the illustrations in this chapter, there are some that capture the desperate personal sadness of living through the Great War. Hundreds of thousands of husbands and fiancés fell on the field of battle; some were never to live long enough to find love. Turn to any issue of *The Illustrated London News* between 1914 and 1918 and the young, handsome faces staring from the weekly Roll of Honour page are a sobering reminder of the transience of love in war.

'The Idol', Arthur Watts, *The Bystander*, 18 November 1914

Caption: *New Recruit: 'By Gad! It's Worth It!'*

Arthur Watts' proud new recruit struts proudly along basking in the quietly admiring glances of a line of chaperoned schoolgirls. This picture was drawn in November 1914, at the end of a period that saw 253,195 men in Great Britain rush to enlist. Magazine illustrations such as this, which bolstered the proud, heroic image of the fighting man, only served to fuel joining-up fever. Watts, a keen sailor before the war, joined the Royal Naval Volunteer Reserve and had a distinguished career, taking part in the attack on Zeebrugge and receiving the DSO.

'Our Wide-Awake Navy – The Perils of Submarine Duty off Folkestone',
Charles Robinson, *The Bystander*, 28 July 1915

A man in a naval uniform was as enticing as one in khaki. The fantasy element of Charles Robinson's work is clear in this picture showing a group of bathing belles emerging like curious mermaids to surround a rather pleased submariner. Before the outbreak of World War I, certain sections of the navy regarded the submarine service as 'no occupation for a gentleman'. Nevertheless, submarines were the first British naval units to go out to face the enemy in 1914 and the last to return to port in 1918; they had significant successes in the Baltic and in the Dardanelles. Submariners soon shook off their ungentlemanlike image (the service raked in 14 Victoria Crosses during the course of the war), prompting Winston Churchill to say, 'Of all the branches of men in the forces, there is none which shows more devotion and faces grimmer perils than the submariners...' (© Estate of Charles Robinson/ILN Picture Library)

'Adoration', Charles Robinson, *The Sketch*, 9 December 1914

Charles Robinson, the elder brother of William Heath Robinson, belonged to the 'fairy school' of illustrators. His lush and florid style was naturally suited to illustrating children's literature (such as Robert Louis Stevenson's *A Child's Garden of Verse*). Nevertheless, romantic and feminine subjects were his forte, as this stylised confection attests. In this, the ultimate idolatry picture, an officer literally stands on a pedestal and accepts the worship of a fashionably plumed lady. It is interesting to note that the majority of fighting men featured in *The Sketch* and *The Tatler* were of officer class, a reflection of the magazines' readership in what was a society starkly divided by class. Significant also was the Roll of Honour published each week in various periodicals and featuring only the names of officers. (© Estate of Charles Robinson/ILN Picture Library)

'Arms and the Man: A suggestion for patriotic girls who wish to show their sympathy with the wounded in a practical way', Edwin Morrow, *The Bystander*, 4 August 1915

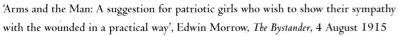

The nifty device in Edwin Morrow's sweet picture reflects an underlying public desire to offer visible support to servicemen, especially wounded ones. Baroness Orczy (author of *The Scarlet Pimpernel*) created the Active Service League, asking women to pledge to persuade men to enlist and 'never to be seen in public with any man who, being in every way fit and free for service, has refused to respond to his country's call'. Soldiers home on leave were always a fascinating prospect for young women, but a wounded soldier had the ultimate cachet.

'Our Lonely Soldiers: The Hon. Mrs. Major de Tomkyns and her daughters make it their duty to take at least one wounded "Tommy" out in their car whenever they go visiting', Charles Robinson, *The Bystander* front cover, 28 July 1915

Many readers of *The Bystander* may have been from the upper classes, but most illustrators were not, and the editors seemed to agree that a little self-deprecating humour would appeal to a wider readership. Here, Charles Robinson's talent for painting the fluid movement of fabrics is exploited to the full, as 'the Hon. Mrs Tomkyns' (a gentrification of Tommy Atkins?) and her daughters shroud a bemused officer in a gauzy flutter of fashionable frills, frocks and parasols. Their altruism is superseded by a peacock display of finery in which their soldier friend is merely an accessory. Although the joke is light-hearted, the underlying message hints that there are more pressing concerns afoot than appearances. (© Estate of Charles Robinson/ILN Picture Library)

Above: 'Man Power', Harold Earnshaw, *The Illustrated Sporting and Dramatic News,*
16 February 1918
Right: 'A Small Objective', Harold Earnshaw, *The Illustrated Sporting and Dramatic News,*
2 November 1918

Although published eight months apart, these two jolly illustrations by Harold Earnshaw make a charming pair. Earnshaw was a well-respected artist, the husband of the more famous Mabel Lucie Atwell. Known as 'Pat' to friends and family, he was an easy-going man with a ready smile. He joined up with the Artists' Rifles in 1915 but lost his right arm on the Somme in 1916. Potentially disastrous for a man who in civilian life had a successful career as an artist, Earnshaw managed to teach himself to draw with his left arm instead. In his own words, 'It may seem strange but the idea of giving up drawing never entered my head'. These pictures, drawn only two years after the loss of his drawing arm, are testament not only to his talent, but also to his determination to overcome a particularly cruel injury. Earnshaw was one of 41,000 British soldiers who lost limbs during World War I. Despite his positive attitude, he was never to recover from the injuries he sustained and died prematurely in 1937. His gravestone is inscribed 'In Memory of Harold Cecil Earnshaw who died from war wounds on March 17th, 1937, aged 51 years'.

'A Mistletoe Nightmare: Awful dream of a very bashful VC on the eve of a Christmas party given in his honour', A. K. Macdonald, *The Bystander*, 27 December 1916

Not all female attention was welcome. As war progressed, the increasing scarcity of men at home provided a regular comedic ingredient for illustrators. A. K. Macdonald specialised in drawing dainty beauties (his later drawings for *The Sketch* in the 1930s are rather saucy), and this ballroom full of giggling, whispering party girls is true to his style. For this nervous Victoria Cross winner, the crème de la crème of eligible chaps, the prospect of entering the room is simply too much.

The Sketch Christmas Number front cover, unattributed artist, 9 December 1914

This unattributed illustration, probably by Archibald Wells, shows a British officer, a Union Jack billowing patriotically in his wake, escorting two stylish ladies. Appearances suggest that the two women may be symbols of Britain's French and Russian allies, bringing a suitably cosmopolitan flavour to a festive issue. Christmas issues of all the *ILN* archive's magazines were lavish affairs, often in colour and each vying to outdo each other. This is a typical example of an early wartime cover, typically upbeat and jaunty, featuring a soldier, a girl on each arm, reaping the rewards of his service with feminine attention.

'Out of the Frying-Pan Into the Fire', William Barribal, *The Sketch*, 9 December 1914

Today, the very thought of a member of the medical profession offering to a light a cigarette for a recovering patient is inconceivable, but in 1914, the discovery and wide acceptance of nicotine's ill effects were still decades away. This picture, by maestro of glamour William Barribal, utilises two potent emblems of romantic illustration – the exchange of a cigarette and the angelic figure of the wartime nurse.

Above: 'Now, Will You Promise', advertisement for Kenilworth cigarettes illustrated by Fred Pegram, *The Tatler*, 19 April 1916

Opposite, left: 'Let's get away from this mob', advertisement for Kenilworth cigarettes illustrated by Fred Pegram, *The Tatler*, 23 May 1917

Up until the Great War, women smokers were a rare breed; they were certainly in existence, but usually among a bohemian minority, and then often practised in secret at home. Society in general disapproved of smoking; the Religious Tract Society even warned in 1898 that

smoking could lead to female moustaches provoked by 'constant movement' of the lips. The social shift brought about by the war allowed women to enjoy a cigarette on a more equal footing, and advertising began to recognise the integral link between smoke and romance. Kenilworth Cigarettes commissioned Fred Pegram to work on a series of advertisements which show alarmingly intimate scenes. Whether engaged in a tender farewell at a railway station, or slipping away from a crowd, Kenilworth remained the constant for Pegram's couple during the long years of conflict. Kenilworth also advertised their delivery service, direct to soldiers at the Front.

'As she took the lighted match from him, their fingers touched', illustration for a short story, 'Delilah', Douglas Mackenzie, *The Bystander*, 27 November 1916

An incidental illustration for a short story, this suggestive picture by Mackenzie portrays a society with more relaxed attitudes to courtship as well as female behaviour, and signals the beginning of smoking as a seductive ritual, which would continue in advertising and celluloid as well as illustration far beyond this war and into the next.

Above: 'In the Black and White Room', Raphael Kirchner, *The Sketch*, 7 June 1916
Right: 'A Feather in her Cap' by Raphael Kirchner, *The Sketch*, 16 June 1915
Opposite left: 'Red, White and Blue', Raphael Kirchner, *The Sketch*, 15 March 1916
Opposite right: 'Bebe', Raphael Kirchner, *The Sketch*, 21 May 1916

World War II may have been the apogee of pin-up art, but it is Raphael Kirchner who can lay claim to be the father of the genre. Born in Vienna, Kirchner attended the Akademie der Bildenden Kunste and moved to Paris around the turn of the century, where his early painting was heavily influenced by the Art Nouveau movement. At the outbreak of war, he moved to the USA, where he continued to produce countless designs for postcards as well as European magazines. Kirchner was the principal artist of *La Vie Parisienne*, and had illustrated many of its covers in the pre-war period. *The Sketch* drew parallels with *La Vie Parisienne*, often referring to it as its 'sister magazine in Paris', although its Gallic

counterpart certainly had a more risqué content. This was exported to Blighty in 1915 when, with a fanfare of trumpets, *The Sketch* announced it was to exclusively publish Kirchner's work in England. The timing was perfect. For thousands of soldiers, the delicate eroticism of Kirchner's beauties provided a welcome relief to the dirt and consistent masculinity of trench life. When portfolios were published by *The Sketch* of Kirchner's work, they sold out in hours, prompting *The Sketch* to warn readers to subscribe in advance for

the next one. The ultimate indicator of Kirchner's popularity must be a picture by Bruce Bairnsfather, published by *The Bystander* in December 1916, showing 'Old Bill' and Bert coming across Bairnsfather's very own homage to the Kirchner Girls, prompting Bill to growl, 'Come on Bert, it's safer in the trenches.' Kirchner died of appendicitis aged only 38, but his legacy lived on in the work of later feted pin-up and glamour artists, notably Alberto Vargas.

'My Hero', William Barribal, *The Illustrated Sporting and Dramatic News*, 26 December 1914
This Barribal girl is a true patriot. Sitting at her desk, she worships at the shrine of her beloved, a selection of Allied flags forming a halo around a photograph of her handsome officer. It's interesting to see the inclusion of a pile of illustrated newspapers in the foreground of the picture, a device included no doubt simply to highlight the fact that the girl is keen to keep abreast of events abroad. However, it's also an indicator of how essential the illustrated periodicals were during World War I as one of the few methods of mass communication.

'Leave', Bruce Bairnsfather, *The Bystander* front cover, 24 May 1916
Abandoning his usual dogged humour, Bruce Bairnsfather, in this surprisingly poignant illustration, shows a snatched moment of tenderness during a soldier's too-short period of leave. Such an emotionally intense period naturally generated a number of marriage proposals.

'A Naval Engagement', Lawson Wood, *The Illustrated Sporting and Dramatic News*, 20 April 1918

This is not the only picture in this chapter with this title, proving an illustrator's love of a military pun! Lawson Wood had an extraordinarily successful career and was well respected in the artistic community. He served in the Kite Balloon Wing of the Royal Flying Corps during the war, observing planes from balloons (an incredibly dangerous undertaking). He was decorated by the French for his action over Vimy Ridge and somehow, like so many other serving artists, he continued to draw throughout the war. (© Estate of Lawson Wood/ILN Picture Library)

'1917's War Wedding', Edwin Morrow, *The Bystander*, 13 December 1916
Accompanied by the following verse:
The woman-worker, smocked and booted, / Will wed the boy that's just recruited;
So, on the land as on the wave, / None but the fair deserve the brave.

Illustrators delighted in exaggerating the skewed male and female roles that resulted from the war. Here, the Women's Land Army (WLA) form a guard of honour for one of their own who is marrying a boyish recruit, several inches shorter than his bride. Efforts to recruit women to work in agriculture had limited success until March 1917 when a new WLA emerged, providing a permanent, skilled female labour force to work on farms, though still not in the numbers hoped for by the government. Smocks and breeches were standard issue but the WLA's own handbook reminded members that despite their mannish attire, they should 'take care to behave like a British girl who expects chivalry and respect from everyone she meets'.

"The Girl They'd Left Behind Them"

SMITH, BROWN, JONES AND ROBINSON THINK OF THE GIRLS THEY LEFT BEHIND THEM,
AND SHOW EACH OTHER THE PHOTOGRAPHS OF THEIR BELOVEDS

'The Girl They'd Left Behind Them', G. L. Stampa, *The Bystander*, 18 August 1915
Photographs of loved ones were often the most precious possession of any serving soldier,
although G. L. Stampa (a regular *Punch* contributor also) prefers to see the funny side,
depicting four rather naïve Tommies realising with dismay that their sweetheart has been rather
too free with her affections.

'A Naval Engagement', G. E. Studdy, *The Bystander*, 24 November 1915
The old adage of 'a girl in every port' gives comic impetus to this picture by George Studdy,
whose sailor's rather promiscuous letter-writing has come to a sticky conclusion at the dock.
Note the obligatory pipe trailing a vapour of smoke upwards. Tobacco had been issued by
the Royal Navy since the early 1800s. World War I saw tobacco rations distributed to all the
armed services, and even though cigarettes were the smoke of choice in the trenches, a sailor
continued to be associated with his pipe. (© George Studdy/ILN Picture Library)

'Till the Boys Come Home', Wilmot Lunt, *The Bystander* Christmas Number, 27 November 1916
Is this a genuinely optimistic and patriotic title, or one with a hidden warning? Certainly, it is not without a hint of irony. The incongruity of two fashionably bedecked women accompanying a wealthy aristocrat to a smart restaurant, while the younger generation are away fighting and others are told to practise austerity, is not lost on the reader. Even *The Times* commented in 1917 that 'there are whole circles of society in which the spirit of sacrifice is unknown', adding that 'There should be no exceptions to the rigorous rule of self-denial which has been willingly undertaken by the great mass of our people' – something this trio plainly appears to have forgotten.

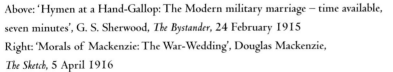

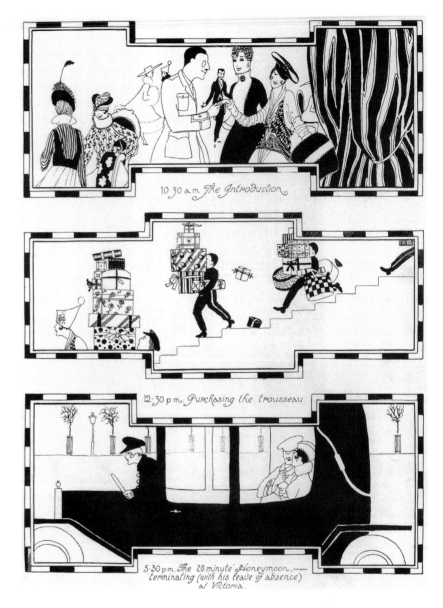

Above: 'Hymen at a Hand-Gallop: The Modern military marriage – time available, seven minutes', G. S. Sherwood, *The Bystander*, 24 February 1915
Right: 'Morals of Mackenzie: The War-Wedding', Douglas Mackenzie, *The Sketch*, 5 April 1916
Young lovers between 1914 and 1918 had no time to lose. Long engagements were definitely out and it was not unknown for couples to get engaged and married in the same period of leave. Although exaggerated for comic effect, these pictures by Douglas Mackenzie and G. S. Sherwood highlight the trend for marrying quickly, even going so far as to suggest that an introduction at 10:30am could easily lead to marriage by lunchtime.

'Great British Victory', Edmund Blampied, *The Bystander*, 16 September 1914

Many romances were denied a happy ending. The enormous, bleak reality of World War I was that over the course of four years of fighting, almost one million men of the British Empire lost their lives – an incalculable loss to society. It is interesting to see such a pessimistic illustration of grief appear at this early stage in the war, and there appears to be little ambiguity over its meaning. The retreat from Mons in late August and the battle of the Marne a few weeks later had resulted in relatively light losses for the British Expeditionary Force, certainly in comparison to those of later battles of the war. Still, almost 3,000 British soldiers had died by the time this picture was published. Rendered in Blampied's elegant, drypoint style, it reflects a scene played over countless times in the living rooms of British homes and quietly conveys the pain of bereavement experienced by thousands of women. (© Estate of Edmund Blampied/ILN Picture Library)

THE WOMAN ABOUT TOWN

Uniforms Smart or Sloppy. War has brought uniforms to women, as to millions of men, who had never an idea of wearing them. As I see them, I think how well worth while it is to have them made at good places. The uniforms turned out in scores are so unbecoming to their wearers, so sloppy and untidy, and in the end not economical because their lives are short. Made by first-rate tailors, such as are found at Jay's, these uniforms are smart and neat, and, being of the very best materials, last much longer. Their wearers take them into their close affections and look after them, and so it is far better war-time economy to have a uniform built at Jay's than half-a-dozen run up somewhere else. As to the good people who air their objection to women wearing khaki, they might just as well object to them making munitions!

The Good Gas. We all know enough about poison gas and the German use of it, but I maintain that we do not know enough of the beneficent gas that is one of the chief treasures of our domestic economy. A little while ago I was staying where coal was £4 a ton. We did without it, and we never missed it, thanks to the good gas which warmed us, cooked our food, and heated our bath-water; and so we gave coal a cold farewell, and warmly welcomed genial gas, with its heat, light, and cleanliness, and its war-time economy.

A Countess Cook. Prince George of Battenberg, who is a nephew of the Tsaritsa, is engaged to a young cousin of the Tsar who, despite her position, has thoroughly studied cookery. She has quite a talent that way, and has made delicacies for invalid soldiers. She is also a mistress of the art of dress, and in her culinary attire looks what Americans would call too 'cute for anything! That cigarettes and cookery do not go harmoniously together is the young Countess's only objection to the profession.

The Language of the Handkerchief. It is not for use —the kind that speaks—but is a dainty little piece of lawn that goes with, or is a striking contrast to, the costume. One sees them beside their harmless, necessary comrades in Robinson and Cleaver's, the creators of the cult of the handkerchief. They have their habitation in a miniature breast-pocket, or are tucked into a smart lapel, and are used for signalling in the code of courtship. It is easier than the Morse code, and the last message, in the first phase, is the accidental dropping of the handkie, which is the beginning of acquaintanceship. Later, I fancy, the code is a secret one; it is, however, quite pretty to watch even by the uninitiated.

properly chosen, properly housed, and properly fed, should produce nine hundred eggs a year! But, if the chickens can't be hatched in bad weather, aren't the hens liable to go on strike if conditions do not please them?

An Art in Dress. Possibly the most difficult of any art in dress is to do real hard work and keep tidy. Lots of women are strenuously employed now, and find the truth of this. The secret of it is suitability. If the dress is suitable to the job, the thing can be done. Of all the obstacles, hair is the worst. A woman's hair may be a glory to her; but it often isn't! Witness the girl 'bus-conductors, the motor-drivers, the trade-tricycle riders, the girl messengers, on wet and windy days: they are neat as new pins, except the hair. Think of the trouble in days of peace to find a becoming golfing-hat which was also practical, or a smart yachting-cap or hat; and now, when women are doing outdoor work in all weathers, it is their worst trouble to manage their hair tidily. If they cut it off and wear caps like men, they are called mannish and unsexed; and if it strays across their faces and into their eyes, they are dubbed unsightly. Personally, the things I have always envied a man most are being able to immerse his head in a basin of water any time he likes, and to wear a hat or cap that fits him. These are, of course, most unfeminine ambitions.

Metal Lace. Our soldiers' and sailors' gold-lace trimmings are reduced to the mere markings of their rank; they look none the less soldierly or sailorly. We women have now taken on a craze for metallic lace of a filmy and fascinating kind. It is used with great effect as trimming for dinner-gowns. We are dressing quite nicely for dinner, even if it is only three courses. It is used for the 'cutest little caps that were ever invented; if we didn't call them caps, they might be taken for rosettes or choux! In dark hair, silver lace; in fair hair, copper lace; in red hair, oxydised lace—I assure you they are most alluring. This lace is not all made in England, but what is not is made by Allies. Nothing so essentially pretty and refined emanates from Frau and Fräulein land, although so many of them are said in German papers to indulge in French fashions—it must, I imagine, be a false allegation. Before the war, when we saw more of them, French dressing is a thing they were never accused of. Frau Frump and Fräulein Dump described most of them quite adequately. It has been found judicious to drop the Frau and have dresses from Paris whenit was a woman's desire to fascinate!

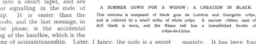

A SUMMER GOWN FOR A WIDOW: A CREATION IN BLACK.
This costume is composed of black gros de Londres and Georgette crêpe, and is relieved by a small collar of white crêpe. A narrow ribbon sash of dull black is worn, and the Ninon veil has a hemstitched border of crêpe-de-Chine.

'A Summer Gown for a Widow: A Creation in Black', Robertson, *The Sketch*, 17 May 1916

During the war, *The Sketch* would run a weekly fashion drawing in each issue, and nothing perhaps reveals the frequency and the untimely nature of death during the Great War better than this suggested outfit for a young widow. Advertisements for mourning clothes had been a regular feature of illustrated journals during the 19th century until the Victorian cult of death gradually began to wane. Nevertheless, mourning clothes, an outward expression of one's inner feelings, were still worn (the death of King Edward VII in 1910 had plunged the majority of the population into black for a time). The outfit is described thus: '…composed of black gros de Londres and Georgette crepe…relieved by a small collar of white crepe. A narrow ribbon sash of dull black is worn, and the Ninon veil has a hemstitched border of crepe-de-Chine.' In reality, no working-class widow would have been able to afford such a sumptuous ensemble.

Up, Up & Away

Land, Sea & Air

While soldiers fought in the mud of the trenches, World War I also transformed the sky and the sea into battlegrounds. Britain was proud of her naval prowess, and ruled the waves in terms of strength and numbers, leading most people to expect that a confrontation at sea in the grand tradition of Trafalgar would be a decisive element of the war. But since the 1890s, Germany, in direct competition with Britain, had embarked on a systematic naval expansion that provoked suspicion among her European neighbours. By 1914, although Britain could boast 30 dreadnoughts to Germany's 20, the latter's increasing naval strength was a worry, and Britain knew that any losses at sea could seriously jeopardise her dominance. This concern informed the decisions of the naval commanders, particularly of Sir John Jellicoe who survived the showdown at the battle of Jutland, and maintained numerical advantage. Britain's conservatism in battle had far-reaching effects. Great naval victories might be prestigious, but by cautiously maintaining numerical superiority, the British navy was able to prolong the blockade of Germany – a strategy with far more harmful consequences than those of a decisive naval victory. While the blockade continued, Germany became hungry.

The pride in Britain's naval strength was exploited by a number of well-known maritime artists, notably Norman Wilkinson and Montague Dawson, who produced several pictures for *The Illustrated London News*, but maritime illustrations were unable to match the illustrative potential of the dashing drama and style of the new kid on the block – the aeroplane.

If Britain dominated the seas, then Germany dominated the air, at least for the first half of the war – by virtue of the far superior fighters which were engineered with 'interrupter gear', a mechanism that allowed bullets to be fired straight through the propeller – though continuing technological developments would see each side enjoy periods of superiority throughout the war.

**'A Crash in the Crater Zone – A Mishap to a Pilot on the Western Front',
Fortunino Matania, *The Sphere*, 27 October 1917**
This wounded pilot has been forced to crash-land, fortunately behind British lines, and despite being wounded, he stays with his plane until help comes. Some German and French pilots carried parachutes in their planes but not the British – the commanders felt they were too bulky and would weigh down the plane. A salvage team has come to help, but of particular interest is the tank seen in the background, painted with a bewilderingly gaudy camouflage.

Aircraft had first been used by the Italians against the Turks in Libya in 1911, and by 1914, the French, British and Germans all had an aerial fighting force. Aeroplanes were proficient multi-taskers; their main role was to drop bombs, which had varying success until the development of strategic bombing craft, but they also provided artillery observation and could make air attacks on the enemy.

The most dramatic subjects for artists were of course the aerial dogfights, in which two planes might duel in mid-air – a fight to the death with the romance of an adventure story. In the air it seemed there was always the opportunity for individual feats of heroism, perfect material for illustrators. As the dashing heroes of the skies, the Royal Flying Corps (RFC) was greatly admired and the flying aces were elevated to god-like status – especially Von Richthofen, the infamous 'Red Baron'. The advent of aviation in war heralded a new area of interest for magazines. *The Bystander* and *The Sphere* regularly brought out a 'Special Aviation Number' both during and after the war.

Another new mode of transport changed the face of war – the tank. The British were pioneers of tank development, and had used armoured cars in Belgium early on in the war. Conscious that wheels would not be able to traverse muddy battlefields, the notion of a tracked vehicle had been mooted early on. It was Winston Churchill, who, along with other military experts, was instrumental in pushing forward the development of such a machine. Thirty-six tanks were first used on the Somme at Flers Courcelette in 1916 but it was the famous Mark IV, some 300 of them, that had moderate success against the Germans at the battle of Cambrai on 20 November 1917. The novelty of these amphibious lumbering monsters did not go unnoticed by illustrators.

Not all forms of transport were mechanised. Quaintly, the Belgians still used dogs to pull their gun carriages, and dogs were frequently used as messengers in the midst of battle. But it was the horse – although in some ways an anachronism in this new age of industrial warfare – that remained an integral element of the Great War. In August 1914, 135,000 horses travelled with the British Expeditionary Force and by 1917, it was estimated that 300,000 horses were with the British army in France, the majority used for transportation or haulage. Many of the more well-heeled readers of the *ILN* magazines would have been horse owners. Some may have even had to give up their horses for the army's needs. Horses were part of the fabric of British life and their role in the war was of enduring interest. It is hardly surprising then that a picture by Fortunino Matania of a gunner bidding farewell to his dying horse, painted for the Blue Cross and published in *The Sphere*, has become one of the most famous sentimental pictures of World War I.

'"The Lion" Turned Slowly And Majestically Round, And Fired Her Broadside-Once',
Montague Dawson, *The Sphere*, 7 December 1914

In the 1960s, the marine artist Montague Dawson was reputed to be the highest paid living painter after Picasso. This picture for *The Sphere* was painted when he was just 24 years old and serving as a lieutenant in the Royal Navy on trawlers and mine-sweepers. Despite great success (he would exhibit for the first time at the Royal Academy just three years later), he continued to paint for *The Sphere* during World War II. Here, Dawson depicts the great 13.5 inch guns of Vice-Admiral Beatty's battlecruiser HMS *Lion* at the battle of Heligoland Bight on 28 August 1914. The action, one of the few offensives by the British at sea, saw the destruction of three enemy light cruisers and one destroyer, while the British got away lightly. The ship did not fare so well at Dogger Bank, 1915, where it was hit repeatedly and damaged severely by the *Moltke*. HMS *Lion* had been built in 1912, and its increased firepower and graceful appearance earned it and other ships in its class the name of the 'splendid cats'.

'Through the Modern Mine-Field: How the Watch is Kept on a Modern Destroyer', D. Macpherson, *The Sphere*, 2 November 1918

A destroyer's crew gingerly negotiate their way through a German-laid minefield in the North Sea. The captain is reading a wireless message and measuring charts while his first lieutenant and navigating officer beyond him keep a sharp lookout. The British Grand Fleet essentially kept the German High Seas Fleet imprisoned in the North Sea, and although major engagements were relatively few and far between (at Dogger Bank, Heligoland and Jutland), the British remained in a state of high alert, maintaining a strategy of cautious self-preservation. Mines were a persistent danger and resulted in the loss of almost 500 Allied and neutral ships during the four years of conflict. Five destroyers, such as the one pictured here, sank as a result of mines, while the cruiser HMS *Hampshire*, en route to Russia with Lord Kitchener on board, hit a mine just 1½ miles off the coast of Orkney with the loss of all on board bar 12 crew members.

'John Travers Cornwell VC at the Battle of Jutland', Fortunino Matania, *The Sphere*, 18 November 1916

One of the most iconic images of heroism and self-sacrifice was that of sixteen-year-old John ('Jack') Travers Cornwell, standing alone at his gun turret position on board the HMS *Chester* during the battle of Jutland on 31 May 1916. Boy Cornwell was sight-setter for one of the guns on the *Chester* which came under fire from four Kaiserliche marine cruisers. He was the sole survivor among his gun crew and remained at his post despite being mortally wounded, dying in hospital in Grimsby shortly after the fleet had returned to England. Various interpretations, invariably sanitised, were published in children's books, and an engraving of Cornwell was even distributed to schools around the country as an example of bravery and devotion. This version by Matania was reproduced after its publication in *The Sphere* in books with rousing titles such as Charles E. Pearce's *Stirring Deeds in the Great War* and G. A. Leask's *Golden Deeds of Heroism*. Cornwell was posthumously awarded the Victoria Cross on 16 September 1916.

'The Sinking of the Giant Cunard Liner, *"Lusitania"*, by a German Submarine', Fortunino Matania, *The Sphere* front cover, 15 May 1915

Matania painted this version of the *Lusitania* disaster from an eyewitness account, conveying the fear, chaos and desperation of the civilian passengers clinging to life while also providing an accurate record of the event. Germany's strategy of unrestricted submarine warfare provoked international outrage when the German U-boat, U-20, commanded by Kapitan-Leutnant Walther Schwieger, fired a single torpedo at the Cunard liner, sinking the ship in 18 minutes with the loss of 1,201 lives including 94 children and, crucially, 128 US citizens. Relatively graphic pictures like this helped to reinforce the strength of public feeling.

'The Missing (Mas) "Cat"', H. M. Bateman, *The Tatler*, 14 August 1918

A warship without a cat wasn't complete and this group of baffled sailors by H. M. Bateman looks decidedly worried. Aside from their practical mouse-catching skills, cats were considered lucky and were even said to predict the weather. After 1975, cats (and all other animals) were banned from Royal Navy vessels on the grounds of hygiene. (© H. M. Bateman Designs Limited/ILN Picture Library)

'"Der Tag" at Last!', Lieut. E. G. O. Beuttler, *The Bystander*, 19 April 1916

Like Arthur Watts, Edward Beuttler was in the Royal Naval Volunteer Reserve, rising to the rank of wing commander by the 1930s. His drawing style is unique and appears far more modern than that of his contemporaries; his strangely chaotic compositions almost verge on the grotesque. Practically all his cartoons for *The Bystander* featured naval life; this one depicts the pell-mell enthusiasm of a crew desperate to see action on 'The Day', after a long period of inactivity. Note the ever-present ship's cat.

'With the French Aviation Service – A Mid-Air Combat', François Flameng, *The Sphere*, 14 September 1918

Planes were first used during the battle of the Marne for reconnaissance duties, but by 1915, opposing aircrews began to attack each other. At first, these tended towards single-handed duels, one pilot pitted against the other in the arena of the skies. Flameng's picture shows a French aviator triumphing as an enemy plane falls in flames, hurtling towards a strangely peaceful looking patchwork of French fields below. The victorious Spad plane is not quite out of danger, having to avoid a hot fire of shrapnel from the enemy's anti-aircraft guns.

'With Our Seaplanes In the North Sea – A Pigeon to the Rescue', W. E. Wigfull, *The Sphere*, 16 November 1918

This broken-down British seaplane in the middle of the North Sea is just one of the beneficiaries of the pigeon's unique homing instinct. The birds were used widely during World War I, with over 100,000 serving as messengers, a staggering 95 per cent of which were successful in reaching their destination. In this case, a small note would be attached to the pigeon requesting help, which would probably arrive in the form of a motor-boat to rescue the stranded aviators.

'The Work of the Royal Air Force During the War: The Development of Formation Fighting', G. H. Davis, *The Sphere*, 1 March 1919

This painting depicts a complex melée of formation fighters circling at different altitudes, the type of tactic that would characterise the latter phase of aerial combat. The 'gaily-painted enemy machines' are probably part of Manfred von Richthofen's famous 'Flying Circus', his four squadrons so named because their pilots chose to paint their planes in bright colours. G. H. Davis was one of the main artists for *The Illustrated London News* in later years, and is particularly well known for his diagrammatic cutaway illustrations during World War II.

'To the Death! – A Glorious Incident of Aerial Warfare on the Western Front', William C. Boswell, *The Tatler*, 27 March 1918

Fighter pilots traded the camaraderie of the trenches for isolated stardom, and, in the case of this picture, the added potential of an indisputably heroic death. The outcome of this dogfight is grim yet 'glorious' in that the British airman, in combat with the famous German pilot Mesinger, realised his plane was in flames and decided to deliberately crash into Mesinger, ensuring that he would bring his opponent down with him. According to *The Tatler*, this knight of the air was part of 'one of the many incidents of heroism and devotion with which the record of the war in the air is so rich'.

'Adieu!: The Wolff Bureau learns that Admiral von Tirpitz has retired with full honours', Alfred Leete, *The Bystander* front cover, 22 March 1916

Admiral Alfred von Tirpitz (1849–1930), creator of the modern German navy, was the mastermind behind its strategy of unrestricted submarine warfare. As Secretary of State of the Imperial Naval Department from the 1890s, Tirpitz embarked on an ambitious ship-building programme, vigorously backed by the Kaiser. By 1914, he was Commander of the German High Seas Fleet, which was still too small to effectively challenge the British. Tirpitz instead placed emphasis on his U-boats, a particularly dishonourable method of warfare in British eyes, and one that met with considerable international disapproval. Admiral von Tirpitz's extraordinary facial hair made him a sitting duck for British caricaturists. He is seen here skulking away wearing medals which commemorate torpedoed ships.

'The Naval Mobilisation: Provisioning a Big Dreadnought', D. Macpherson, *The Sphere*, 8 August 1914

This fascinating insight into the supplies needed for one month at sea for the 900-strong crew of a British dreadnought (the most advanced type of big gun battleship) is not only impressive in its quantities, but also reveals how tastes and diets have changed over the years. 1,000 boxes of cigarettes would definitely not be supplied today, but neither would 15 boxes of bloaters, 8 cases of tongue or 12 cases of tinned brawn. Most interesting is the 2 cwt of German sausage heading for the hold. The revolutionary *Dreadnought*, first launched in 1906, was a turbine-powered, all-big-gun warship which outclassed all existing capital ships.

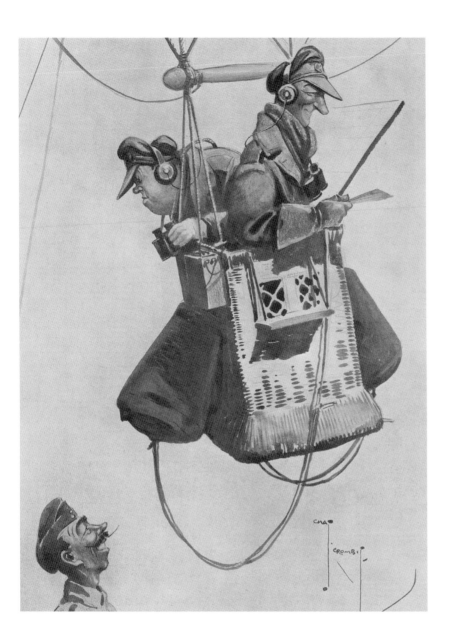

'The Old Order Changeth – "Flight Sergeant, In Future When We Go Up, Just give The Order 'Let Go', instead of 'Let Go The Guys'"', Charles Crombie, *The Illustrated Sporting and Dramatic News*, 21 September 1918

Kite balloons, which were used for observation and controlled by a cable attached to the ground, were often known as 'sausages'. They had been used by both the naval and military wings of the air service, but were automatically transferred to the control of the RAF on its formation in the spring of 1918 (the caption to this picture no doubt refers to an accompanying change of parlance). Suspended in mid-air in a wicker basket with only a parachute as a means of escape, observation balloonists were extremely vulnerable and often subject to attacks by enemy aircraft.

'The Swan Song of Richthofen', Hawley Morgan, *The Illustrated Sporting and Dramatic News*, 4 May 1918

The renown of Manfred von Richthofen, better known as the Red Baron, was legendary. The ultimate fighter ace, he took command of Jagdstaffel 1, flying a distinctive red Fokker DR-1 which struck fear into the hearts of the British pilots he hunted down. On 21 April 1918 he was brought down and killed, either by the Sopwith Camels of the Royal Air Force he was engaged with, or an Australian machine gunner on the ground – the debate continues. At the time of his death he had shot down 80 enemy aircraft, more than any other ace. Richthofen was buried with full honours by his British enemies, a common practice among airmen.

'With the French Aviation Service – A Night Bombardment by a Voisin Biplane',
François Flameng, *The Sphere*, 14 September 1918

French artist François Flameng had already established success by the time war broke out.
He was a professor at the Paris Academy of Fine Arts, had designed France's first bank notes,
and received the Legion d'Honneur. Most of his illustrations appeared in *L'Illustration*, but
many were also reproduced in *The Sphere*. He was one of the foremost French war illustrators,
though often criticised for his lack of drama. However, it is his restraint that has left us with
some of the most believable images of the war.

Early bombing raids were of limited success and further advances were necessary to improve
accuracy. However, this set-up, though perhaps crude to modern eyes, was sophisticated
technology in 1918.

'An Exciting Moonlight Encounter between Motor-Cycle Despatch Rider and a Party
of Uhlans', Christopher Clark, *The Sphere*, 12 December 1914

The Belgian despatch rider who is the subject of this illustration by Christopher Clark (a
'special artist' for *The Sphere*) escaped a party of German Uhlans (lancers) by the skin of his
teeth on his 7 horsepower 'Indian' motorcycle. With bullets whistling around him, the rider
(referred to as E. van Isacker) managed to outpace the pursuing Germans before crashing his
motorcycle and losing consciousness. The American-made 'Indian' motorcycle held every
American speed and distance record by 1911, but the makers brought a halt to racing during
the war when they supplied 41,000 motorcycles to the Front.

Left: 'Goodbye Old Man', Fortunino Matania, *The Sphere*, 24 June 1916

Above: 'His Pains on Our Behalf', C. J. Payne, *The Graphic*, 9 January 1915

Despite the technological strides taken during World War I, horses remained an essential element of the war effort. They were used by mounted infantry, in cavalry charges and, more prosaically, for moving men and goods. Many of the Yeomanry volunteer regiments brought their mounts with them, a decision that often made parting with their wounded or dead animals difficult to bear.

One of the most famous paintings of World War I, and almost certainly Fortunino Matania's best-known work, is 'Goodbye Old Man', subtitled 'An incident on the road to battery position in Southern Flanders'. The picture, showing a heartbreaking farewell between a gunner and his horse, was commissioned in 1916 by the Blue Cross Fund to raise money to relieve the suffering of war horses in Europe. This was no minor charitable campaign – over one million horses saw service with the British army through the course of the war and the Blue Cross treated thousands. The picture was also the apparent model for the 58th Division memorial near Amiens. The picture by C. J. Payne shows Blue Cross men rounding up injured horses to be returned to depot. Horses injured beyond hope would be humanely destroyed. Matania's picture was reproduced in a large number of magazines – *The Illustrated London News* produced a special print for its readers – as well as on postcards, and remains a popular, if sentimental, symbol of the Great War even today.

Above: 'A Forecast of the Mobile Land Forts Now Being Used on the Western Front', G. Bron, from a sketch in the *New York World*, *The Sphere*, 23 November 1916

Right: 'A Tale of Two Tanks', W. Heath Robinson, *The Illustrated Sporting and Dramatic News*, 10 February 1917

Opposite page: 'Can-Tank-erous', Bruce Bairnsfather, *The Bystander*, 11 April 1917

Caption: *''Ere! Where the 'ell are ye comin' with that Turkish bath o' yours?'*

Tanks were first used at Flers Courcelette on the Somme on 15 September 1916. Despite their slow speed and inefficiency, they apparently terrified the Germans. Images of this action did not appear in *The Sphere* until two months after the event, and in the intervening period, people speculated on what the mechanised monsters reported in despatches might look like. The war correspondent Philip Gibbs described them as 'motor-monsters…crawling forward to the rescue'. This adaptation of a sketch from an American newspaper conjures up a futuristic scene of gloomy Armageddon, with mechanised behemoths – imaginatively named 'trench tractors' and 'electric gyro-cruisers' in *The Sphere* – lurching through the war-torn landscape. By contrast, Heath Robinson and Bruce Bairnsfather thankfully treat the subject of tanks with their usual flippancy. (Heath Robinson image © Mrs J. C. Robinson by kind permission of the proprietor and Pollinger Limited/ILN Picture Library)

'The Day'

Victory & Peace

In an issue of *The Bystander* dated 20 November 1918, weekly columnist 'Blanche' ruminated on Britain's new-found peaceful state:

And it is, too, the right peace — peace with honour, peace with victory, the peace our brave men fought and died for, the peace we have sacrificed, oh! What irreplaceable treasure to regain. But it has come, of course, to a world that's not at all the same old world as the gay, untried, untroubled one it forsook in August, 1914.

She spoke for many. A year earlier in November 1917, Lord Lansdowne, a very senior Tory politician, writing in the letters column of the *Daily Telegraph*, had first mooted the possibility of negotiating peace, but his suggestion was met with scorn by a public who felt that the endured years of hardship and loss could only be justified by total victory. G. K. Chesterton argued in *The Illustrated London News* that a compromise would only encourage the spread of Prussianism:

They would glorify not our sword, but his shield. The superstition that the soldier of North Germany is unconquerable and therefore (by his own philosophy) infallible, would be much more firmly established than if there had never been a war at all.

By 1918, both sides were being asked to dig deeper and fight harder than ever. With Russia out of the war, a million German troops were freed up to launch the crushing German spring offensive, an operation that nearly won the war. Haig asked everything of his men in words that became legendary;

Every position must be held to the last man. . . With our backs to the wall, and believing in the justice of our cause, each one of us must fight on to the end.

Victory, the only course that would gratify the British public, was swift when it came. The arrival of the Americans had intensified the Allied endeavour, but it was the faltering of the enemy offensive that proved to

'Roses of Victory', Claude Shepperson, *The Tatler*, 1 March 1919
A mood of elegant romance permeated Claude Shepperson's pictures and his confident use of space added grandeur to pictures that would have otherwise been simply an artistic delicacy. The effect gives a pleasant balance between the victorious troops marching towards the horizon and the girl waving to them.

be the turning point. The Germans had been too fast for their supplies to keep up and the advance suffered when, impeded by hunger, German troops stopped to gorge themselves on food left in the British lines. At the battle of Belleau Wood in June 1918, the American soldiers laid to rest any doubts on the bravery of their troops, and as the Allied offensive gained momentum in August – in the so-called 'Hundred Days' – General Ludendorff began to lose faith, calling 8 August, a day when British Empire troops inflicted a crushing defeat on the enemy, 'the black day of the German Army'.

By September 1918, German morale was at a low ebb. Most soldiers simply wanted the war to be over. Beginning on 26 September, the Allies began a series of sequential attacks along the entire length of the Western Front, from Ypres in the North to the Verdun area. 29 September, when British (along with Australian and American) troops of the Fourth Army broke the Hindenburg Line, was a crucial day. Ludendorff told Hindenburg they should seek an armistice. On 25 October he was forced to resign.

In the two weeks between Ludendorff's resignation and the abdication of the Kaiser on 9 November, the entwined Alliances of the Central Powers collapsed like a house of cards. Turkey surrendered on 30 October, and Austria-Hungary on 3 November. With its people close to revolution at home, Germany finally admitted defeat. Early on 11 November, in a railway carriage in a forest clearing close to Compiègne, Germany agreed to the Allied peace terms, and the Armistice came into effect at the eleventh hour of the eleventh day of the eleventh month.

Around the world, the news was greeted with jubilation. Shops and schools were hurriedly closed and millions thronged the streets in spontaneous celebration. And yet alongside the joy there was pain and sadness and the pressing knowledge that life would never be the same again: 614,000 British servicemen, 145,000 merchant seamen and 1,117 British civilians had died in the war. Overall, a million of the British Empire's population had lost their lives, and despite the survivors who returned home, to those who had lived through the last four years it seemed as if a whole generation of young men was gone, an incalculable loss to society. For the families who had lost husbands, brothers and sons, the victory celebrations must have been streaked with a poignant bitterness, making the process of remembrance and commemoration especially important. Over 600 cemeteries in Northern France were eventually constructed on land deeded in perpetuity by the French government for that purpose. In response to public demand, memorials were erected in almost every town and village up and down the country. Ninety years on the remembrance continues.

The country the survivors returned to – Lloyd George's 'land fit for heroes' – was unable to meet their expectations. The national debt led to high taxation and increasing inflation, housing was in short supply and rationing continued well into 1920. The class distinctions that had defined pre-war British society had been shaken but only slightly: despite a massive loss of wealth by the aristocracy, two-thirds of the nation's assets were still owned by less than three per cent of the population. Women who had been left widowed by the war found it difficult to manage on the meagre war widow's pension, and some of the jobs that women had filled during the war once again became a male preserve. However, the war had given women a chance to show what they could do, and far more women than before were employed in clerical jobs.

For a while, the post-war era was a boom time; wages had doubled and the average working week was reduced. But the economic difficulties of the country could not be ignored and the socio-political landscape of the 1920s was punctuated by strikes and industrial disputes.

What did the end of the war mean for magazine artists? All the magazines that became the 'Great Eight' in the 1920s survived the war to prosper during the inter-war era. Bruce Ingram, the editor of *The Illustrated London News*, returned from France to his desk in 1918 and stayed there until 1964, a record-breaking tenure. Magazine art continued to flourish. Better printing techniques allowed more regular full-colour pages, a progression that showcased the work of artists such as Bateman, Barribal, Blampied, the Robinson brothers and Lewis Baumer. The 'Peace' issues published by the magazines to coincide with the 1919 Treaty of Versailles were lavish affairs crammed with colour illustrations, as if colour had once more entered people's lives after the drab days of khaki. It would take another war to sound the death knell of magazine illustration; for the time being, it was very much alive and well.

'In Germany – Now', Wilmot Lunt, *The Bystander*, 10 January 1917

Caption: *Member of the queue: 'Yes – that's the Food Dictator who tells us how much we've got to eat'*

By 1917, the German population was beginning to feel the pinch. Whereas the British had managed to survive the U-boat blockade by organising their merchant fleet into convoys, the Allied blockade of Germany had been ruthlessly effective, and the country came close to starvation. The situation was no better for the German army when no meat or fresh produce was available. Hunger in Germany was certainly a deciding factor in the eventual Allied victory and this queue of Germans, glowering at the astounding girth of the man who has no compunction in telling them 'Wurst Verboten', sends an important message to British readers.

'Battered, But Victorious', Fortunino Matania, *The Sphere* front cover, 14 September 1918

Between 8 August, Germany's 'black day' on which the Allies broke the line at Amiens, and the Armistice on 11 November, the British army won a series of decisive victories that ranks among the greatest in its history, yet is often overshadowed by the horrors of the battles of the Somme and Passchendaele. The courage and endurance of the front-line soldiers was complemented by ever-improving technological and tactical backup from tanks, aircraft, wireless, intelligence and mechanised weaponry. During the 'Hundred Days', the British army took 188,700 prisoners and 2,840 guns. Matania's picture seems to capture the impending sense of a final, conclusive struggle.

'Some Guy', Frank Newbould, *The Bystander* **front cover, 6 November 1918**
Published just five days before peace was declared, this American soldier's torch says it all: 'Unlimited manpower'. When the US troops began to arrive in Europe, their plump, fresh appearance earned them the nickname of 'doughboys', but their ferocious fighting spirit and sheer numbers soon began to overwhelm the Germans. As well as a 'black and white' illustrator, Frank Newbould was a well-known poster artist who produced designs for the LNER train company. He also worked as assistant to Abram Games, producing some of World War II's finest propaganda posters.

'The Next Haig Convention', Arthur Ferrier, *The Bystander* **front cover, 23 October 1918**
By 23 October, Britain could almost taste victory and this picture by Arthur Ferrier, showing a cowed Kaiser handing over his sword to Douglas Haig, would be frighteningly accurate if it were not for the fact that the Allies demanded the Kaiser's abdication before they would discuss armistice terms. 'Little Willie', the Kaiser's eldest son, and the bulk of Hindenburg complete a fairly dejected trio. Arthur Ferrier led a colourful life. Born in Scotland, he began his career as an analytical chemist, before becoming a cartoonist at the *Daily Record* in Glasgow. His move to London saw him contribute to *Punch*, *London Opinion* and *Tit-Bits* as well as *The Bystander* and *The Sketch* in later years. He is best known for pioneering the glamorous cartoon-strip girl, and illustrating 1940s and 50s theatreland. A great socialite and raconteur, his *Times* obituary referred to him as a 'cartoonist, portrait painter, bon viveur and wit'.

'The Lighter Side', Bernard Hugh, *The Bystander*, 1 January 1919

Caption: *Tommy (on furlough pending discharge): 'Blimey, I should fancy I had my bathing-costume on'*

A soldier returning home weighed down with a greatcoat, boots, rifle, rucksack and (in the case of this particular man) a number of Christmas presents, must have found civvies a strangely enlightening experience. Demobilised soldiers could choose to keep their greatcoats or to hand them back to the army in return for a payment of £1.

'Over the Top', Bernard Hugh, *The Bystander*, 8 January 1919

The demobilisation of the army was a slow process, as this picture from January 1919 confirms. Some units remained to police the Rhineland region, and were topped up by regulars, but the rest would be divided up for demobilisation according to priority. Civil servants – the ones who would administer the return of so many men to the workforce – went first, followed by 'pivotal men' (the job creators) and then 'slip men' (who had notes from employers promising work). The system was flawed, allowing more recent recruits to 'demob' earlier than longer serving soldiers, but after the 1918 General Election, the process became speedier.

'Good-bye-e-e!', Harold Earnshaw, *The Bystander*, 11 December 1918
These girls marching off to pastures new seem a jolly bunch, although for the 750,000 women who found themselves suddenly unemployed in 1919, the choices of 'new jobs' were very limited. Women who were made redundant were given two weeks' pay in lieu of notice, and their train ticket home. Subsequently, they would receive six months' unemployment benefit, although those who chose to remain on benefit rather than accept available work – usually domestic service – were the subject of virulent contempt. Those women who continued in employment, particularly if married, were accused of being greedy, only holding onto men's jobs in order to earn themselves a little 'pin money'. Women did continue to be employed in clerical and shop work after the war, but, broadly speaking, both sexes were complicit in steering a return to pre-war gender roles and employment patterns.

Above: 'Unbullying beef left over from the war', W. Heath Robinson, *The Bystander*,
15 January 1919

Right: 'A Mere Matter of Form. Distressing mistake of a cook recently released from
a munition factory', W. Heath Robinson, *The Illustrated Sporting and Dramatic News*,
25 January 1919

When the war ended, Heath Robinson remarked on how once more he was called upon to
adapt his work to the changing conditions: 'Peace, reconstruction and demobilisation were
among the subjects I treated. Reconstruction, especially in the war zones, was a fruitful subject
for humorous drawings.' The notion of having once again to rearrange and reorganise appealed
to the Heath Robinson sense of humour, where the tortuous and elaborate would always be
chosen over the simple and straightforward. 'Unbullying' beef was particularly popular: the
tins of bully beef that had seen Tommy through the war were pointlessly and painstakingly
reconstituted into good old joints of British beef. (© Mrs J. C. Robinson by kind permission
of the proprietor and Pollinger Limited/ILN Picture Library)

'A Christmas Visitor', Fred Pegram, *The Sphere*, 30 November 1918

Fred Pegram, a cousin of H. M. Brock, was particularly fond of playing the innocent voyeur and is a sensitive observer of the emotional intimacy between men and women. There is something of the 'happy ever after' about this picture, which shows a woman interrupted in her Christmas decorating by the unexpected arrival of her wounded lover from the Front. As she turns to look, the soft winter sunshine floods in through the open door and bathes the returning hero in a light which, purposefully or not, recalls a religious visitation.

'Christmas Leave', Herbert Pizer, *The Bystander* Annual, 1918
Caption: *(If the Germans Had Won), But On This Page They Jolly Well Haven't (Ed.)*
This colourful party scene by Herbert Pizer formed part of a cheeky celebratory issue of *The Bystander* entitled, 'If the Germans Had Won'. The scene is more 1920s than World War I, with the flirty dresses and bobbed hair of the ladies in attendance. Pizer's style and subject matter is very similar to that of William Barribal – both men painted glamorous, ravishing women, rendered with rapid brush strokes in vivid hues. As well as work for *The Bystander*, he also painted a number of covers for the short-lived but glamorous 1920s magazine, *Pan*.

'Armistice Week Rejoicings in the West End: The Scene at Piccadilly Circus', Fortunino Matania, *The Sphere*, 23 November 1918

Fortunino Matania's impression of victory celebrations in London's Piccadilly Circus is to be admired not only for its detail, but for the speed with which he produced it – peace was declared on 11 November and this picture was published just 12 days later. Amongst the hubbub are an American sailor waving his crutch in victory, nurses, French and Highland soldiers, packed open-top buses, flags draped out of windows all the way up Regent Street and a small dog wearing a Pickelhaube helmet. It is a joyous composition and an apt conclusion to the huge body of work Matania produced for *The Sphere* during the war years.

'Henley – "After the War"', Charles Sykes, *The Bystander*, 23 May 1917

Caption: *How to use up any remnants of the German Fleet that may be left over after the Navy has had a real chance at them*

Messing about with boats is the optimistic theme of this illustration from 1917, showing the despised German U-boat fleet 're-commissioned' after the war at Henley.

'Futurist Fiction', Bruce Bairnsfather, *The Bystander*, 4 December 1918

Caption: *Of course, there is no doubt the war will affect romantic fiction. Extract from a 1944 magazine story: 'Raising her gas-mask, he raided her mud-stained crater-like mouth with a barrage of kisses'*

Bairnsfather's power of foresight is uncanny in this picture, showing two lovers wearing gas masks. Little did Bairnsfather know that just two decades later, lovers would be carrying and wearing real gas masks, not just those in a novelist's imagination.

'Fame Visits the Heroic Unknown Dead', Fortunino Matania, *The Sphere*, 13 November 1920

As part of the commemoration process in the immediate aftermath of the war, a body was exhumed from one of the major fields of battle on the Western Front and brought back to England where it was interred in the west end of the nave of Westminster Abbey, representing all those who had fought and died in the Great War, particularly those with no known grave. In the week following the ceremony on 11 November 1920, an estimated 1,250,000 people visited the tomb of the unknown warrior to pay their respects. It remains one of the most visited war graves in the world. The inscription on the tomb is from the Bible: 'They buried him among the Kings, because he had done good toward God and toward his house.' (2 Chronicles 24:16)

Above: 'The Hun Helmet', Reginald Higgins, *The Bystander*, 6 November 1918
Right: 'Bye-Bye Khaki', Reginald Higgins, *The Tatler*, 5 March 1919

For the bohemian, fashionable young thing, what better way to use a war souvenir than as a hanging basket? Several years later, Reginald Higgins exhibited a group of paintings under the title 'Some Modern Girls' at the Sporting Gallery in London's Covent Garden. A *Times* review gave short shrift to his vision of the modern girl: 'These girls have no roots in reality. What Mr Higgins has done very cleverly and with considerable decorative charm, is to draw the convention of the modern girl created by letters to "the papers" and the less perceptive kind of novel. As designs they may please anyone; as types they will only convince people who live in a world of illusion – or Hampstead when the shops are closed.' So, perhaps the new woman as portrayed by Reginald Higgins did not exist. I prefer to think otherwise, but either way, this witty treatment of a German helmet, or the blasé way a lady in her boudoir kisses farewell to her khaki uniform, seems to sum up the carefree spirit of victory.

'Viewing the Battlefields', Fortunino Matania, *The Sphere*, 20 September 1919
The aftermath of the war saw a wave of tourists visiting the battlefields of France and Belgium. A combination of memory, personal experience and nationalistic urge prompted people to make these pilgrimages. Just as a visit today to one of the immaculately tended cemeteries of France is still a moving experience, sites like the shattered ruins of Ypres in this Matania painting must have had a powerful impact in 1919.

'Keeping Green the Memory of "The Glorious Dead": Brotherhood in Sorrow at the Whitehall Cenotaph', A. Forestier, *The Illustrated London News, 2 August 1919*

In contrast to the rampant joy in Matania's picture depicting victory celebrations in London, the prevailing emotion in this illustration by Amédée Forestier is one of quiet reflection and communal sadness. The *ILN* editorial stressed how 'all classes mingled in a common tribute to their fallen heroes' at Lutyens's memorial to the Glorious Dead. In 1919, the cenotaph was temporarily constructed out of wood and plaster, but such was the public enthusiasm for the monument, it was completed the following year in Portland stone and remains the central focus for the Remembrance Day ceremony nine decades on.

'Complete Surrender', H. H. Harris, *The Bystander* Christmas Number,
4 December 1918

The Bystander demonstrated how delighted it was with victory with a peacock display of colour
pages in its Christmas number for 1918, such as this one by H. H. Harris, another artist who
designed covers for *Pan* magazine, and continued to supply magazines with a succession of
beaming, brightly hued pin-ups during the 1920s. Harris is perhaps best known for his famous
Bovril advertisement with the caption 'Prevents that sinking feeling'.

The Tatler Peace No. front cover, by Annie Fish ('Fish'), *The Tatler*, 5 March 1919
This bold cover design for *The Tatler*'s Peace number is by Annie Fish, who simply signed
herself 'Fish'. Fish was one of *The Tatler*'s regulars, illustrating the weekly column 'Letters of
Eve' (written by Mrs Maitland Davies) with her decorative pen and ink style. *The Tatler*, along
with *The Sketch* and *The Bystander*, repeatedly published pictures of dressing up and parties as the
prevailing symbols of peace in their immediate post-war issues.

PEACE ON EARTH
GOODWILL TOWARDS
MEN

'Once Upon a Time', Bruce Bairnsfather, *The Bystander*, 25 December 1918

What did Old Bill do after the war? He sat by his hearth in a comfortable armchair and puffed on his pipe in quiet contemplation. The charm of Bairnsfather's Old Bill creation lay in his innate humanity – that familiar mix of grumpy sarcasm and vulnerability. It is the latter emotion that is visible here, a scene which would have been familiar in living rooms throughout the country. Men might return to their pipe and slippers but they also lived with the memories of the trenches and of dead friends. Very few spoke about it. Writing again in *The Bystander*, 'Blanche' summed up the mood: 'One does not go down into the deep, dark waters of grief or dwell for weary months and years in the shadow of fear and come out into the light of day again QUITE the same; and men do not wound and kill and see appalling sights and change their whole way and manner of life and remain as before these unusual happenings.'

Glossary of Illustrators

Below are short biographies covering a selection of the artists in this book. Further biographical information on these and other illustrators can be found within the captions in the main body of the book.

ATTWELL, Mabel Lucie (1879–1964)

Born on 4 June 1879 in Mile End, London, Attwell was the daughter of a butcher and the ninth of ten children. She studied art at Heatherley's School of Art and St Martin's School of Art (where she met her husband, Harold Earnshaw) but disliked formal training and completed neither course. Best known for her inimitable drawings of chubby, endearing children, her early work was accepted for publication by *The Bystander* and *The Tatler* (she continued to provide occasional drawings for the latter after World War I) and she designed her first poster for London Underground in 1906. A prolific worker, Attwell's drawings appeared on hundreds of postcards for Valentine's of Dundee, in children's books (including an edition of *Peter Pan and Wendy*, and *Peeping Pansy* written by Queen Marie of Romania), on posters, plaques and all kinds of ephemera. She moved to Fowey in Cornwall where she died in 1964. She remains one of Britain's best-loved and most collectible illustrators.

BAIRNSFATHER, Charles Bruce (1887–1959)

Born in Muree, India, the son of an army officer, Bairnsfather served in the Royal Warwickshire Regiment before leaving the army to study at John Hassall's New Art School. He worked for an electrical engineering firm but re-joined his regiment with the outbreak of war, where he rose from the rank of second lieutenant to captain. In 1915, *The Bystander* began to publish the drawings Bairnsfather sent from the Front depicting the humorous side of trench life and featuring the central character of 'Old Bill'. The success of 'Fragments from France' made Bairnsfather into a household name, and his cartoons were considered so morale-boosting that he was made Officer Cartoonist in the Intelligence Department. He was also engaged by the French, Italian, Australian and US governments to produce cartoons of their respective armies. The success of Bairnsfather's cartoons sustained his career beyond the war as a comic artist, writer, playwright, lecturer and performer. During World War II he was Official War Artist to the US Army and his illustrations continued to be published in *The Bystander* until it merged with *The Tatler* in 1940.

BARRIBAL, William H. (1873–1956)

William Barribal was born in London and apprenticed to a lithographic printer before travelling to Paris, where he studied at the Academie Julian (Kirchner was briefly one of his fellow students). He was predominantly a figurative and portrait painter and is best known for his ravishing beauties, which appeared in magazines, particularly *The Bystander* and *Holly Leaves*, and in advertising and promotional material for companies like Schweppes. He also designed a popular set of playing cards for Waddingtons. A member of both the Savage and the London Sketch Club, he was president of the latter from 1931 to 1932. Barribal, known as 'Barri' to his peers, was great friends with Bruce Bairnsfather and painted a portrait of him, which was exhibited at the Royal Academy Summer Exhibition in 1917. Barribal's pin-ups were based on a number of models, but their porcelain skin and rosebud lips all bore a resemblance to his wife Babs, who was intensely jealous of the young women who frequented her husband's studio.

Barribal exhibited regularly from 1920 to 1960, including at the Walker Art Gallery in Liverpool and the Royal Academy. He joined the Artists' Rifles in 1914 but did not see active service, probably due to an injured hand which he nevertheless managed to draw with.

BATEMAN, Henry Mayo (1887–1970)

H. M. Bateman was born in New South Wales in Australia to English parents, who returned to London when he was two years old. A prodigious talent, the artist Phil May, who was a prominent illustrator at *The Graphic*, admired his early cartoons and encouraged him to pursue an artistic career. After studying at Westminster School of Art and Goldsmith's Institute in New Cross, South London, he worked in the studio of Charles Van Havenmaet before his first work began to be published. Some of the earliest was in *The Tatler* in 1904, beginning a relationship that would span three decades. Bateman's drawings were inimitable: lively, vigorous and occasionally scathing. His confident, efficient style revolutionised British comic illustration – by his own admission he 'went mad on paper'. During his long career he contributed to *The Tatler*, *The Sketch* and *The Bystander*, as well as *Punch*. He was at the height of his powers in the 1930s, producing 'The Man Who' series for *The Tatler*, in which he depicted a parade of haughty society matrons, blustering colonels and snivelling subalterns as players in a series of social faux pas. Bateman died in Gozo in 1970.

BAUMER, Lewis Christopher Edward (1870–1963)

Lewis Baumer was born and brought up in St John's Wood and was encouraged by his parents to attend art school there before stints at the South Kensington and Royal Academy schools. An artistic protagonist of the 'bright, young things', with a warm, effervescent style, he began working for *Punch* in 1920 where he was one of their best-loved social commentators. For *The Bystander* and *The Tatler*, Baumer produced a number of attractive oil and pastels of the modern-day flapper girl.

BLAMPIED, Edmund (1886–1966)

Perhaps Jersey's most famous artist, Blampied, the son of a French-speaking farmer, showed a talent for drawing from an early age. Speaking the bare minimum of English, he left Jersey in 1903 to attend Lambeth School of Art and then found work making topical pen and ink sketches for *The Daily Chronicle*. A gold medal at the 1925 Paris Exposition for his lithography ensured a string of commissions and he was a prolific illustrator of books and magazines. He is best known for his work in etching and drypoint, but he also worked in oils, watercolour, pencil and was an accomplished sculptor. He is feted for his rural scenes of Jersey, but his work for the *ILN*, *The Sphere* and *The Bystander* – for which he did a number of gorgeous watercolours of glamorous society around the globe rendered in his elegant, fluid style – shows an artist able to turn his hand to most subjects.

BROCK, Henry Matthew (1875–1960)

H. M. Brock was the younger brother of Charles Edmund Brock and studied at Cambridge School of Art. Unlike his brother, he worked almost exclusively in pen and ink, and his rapid-fire, dramatic sketches suited him well to illustrating boys' adventure stories. As well as illustrating numerous books including Robert Louis Stevenson's *Treasure Island* and Charles Kingsley's *Westward Ho!*, he contributed to most of the illustrated magazines, including all the *ILN* magazines. He shared a studio with his elder brother C. E. Brock, where they assembled a large number of props used for historical illustrations in works by Dickens, Austen and Thackeray.

BUCHANAN, Fred Charles (1878–1941)

Fred Buchanan served with the Artists' Rifles during World War I, along with Harold Earnshaw, James Thorpe and Bert Thomas. He was a regular contributor to *Punch* and *The Strand* as well as a popular postcard artist. He was a long-term member of Ilford Dramatic Society and as a fine singer and practical joker, his talents were much in demand at Sketch Club social occasions.

CUNEO, Cyrus Cincinnato (1879–1916)

Cuneo is a fascinating figure who came to a tragic end. The father of the more famous painter Terence Cuneo, Cyrus was an Italian-American flyweight boxing champion who used his prize money to travel to Paris and study art under Whistler. He arrived in London in 1903, finding success as an illustrator of various subjects, but particularly of royal ceremonials. When war broke out the proceeds from an auction of one of his canvases were enough to buy two ambulances for the Front, each bearing the inscription 'The Cyrus Cuneo Ambulance'. At the age of 37 and at the peak of his career, Cuneo died of blood poisoning after being scratched by a lady's hat pin at a dance.

DOWD, James H. (1884–1956)

J. H. Dowd's fluent brush strokes were particularly suited to drawing children and he illustrated a large number of children's books. He also was a contributor to *Punch* from 1906, later becoming their first film cartoonist. During the war, he served as an orderly for the Royal Army Medical Corps at the 3rd London Wandsworth Hospital, where he, along with H. M. Bateman and C. R. W. Nevinson, contributed to the hospital's prestigious magazine, *The Gazette*.

EARNSHAW, Harold Cecil (1886–1937)

Harold Earnshaw, known as 'Pat', was born in Woodford, Essex in 1886. His grandfather was Rector of Sheffield University and his father, Frederick, had left Yorkshire to join a firm of scientific instrument-makers in the south. He met Mabel Lucie Atwell while studying at St Martin's School of Art in Central London, and the pair married in June 1908. A talented artist in his own right, Pat often painted the less 'Atwellish' part of his wife's paintings, such as animals or scenery. He was a member of the London Sketch Club and good friends with the artists Harry Rountree and Bert Thomas, with whom he regularly played golf. In 1915, he joined the Artists' Rifles and was at the Somme in 1916 when he lost his right arm. He learned to draw with his left arm and continued his career as before, contributing to *The Tatler* and *The Bystander* as well as illustrating numerous books. He never fully recovered from his war injuries and died in 1937.

FISH, Annie (1890–1964)

Annie Fish was born in Bristol, before her family moved to Ealing in West London. She was home-taught and then studied art at John Hassall's School of Art under George Belcher. Having contributed to American *Vogue* and *Vanity Fair*, she began to contribute to *The Sketch* in 1914, but she is best known for her illustrations in *The Tatler*, to accompany their society column, 'Letters of Eve', written by Mrs Maitland Davies. The formula of witty gossip and Fish's decorative black and white illustrations spawned imitators in *The Sketch* and *The Bystander*. The influence of Aubrey Beardsley is clear from her work, with its two-dimensional, stylised figures, and cross-hatching or dots to convey the flounces, frills and powder puffs which artistically littered *The Tatler*'s 'Eve' pages each week. She was also a prolific commercial artist and created advertisements for Abdullah cigarettes and Erasmic soap among others. A consummate designer, she worked on textile designs for her husband, Walter William Sefton, who was a Belfast linen manufacturer. She was a member of a number of clubs and artistic societies but retired to the artistic colony of St Ives in Cornwall in the 1940s to concentrate on painting.

FORESTIER, Amédée (1854–1930)

Forestier joined the staff of *The Illustrated London News* as a 'special artist' in 1882, covering predominantly ceremonial and state occasions in Britain, Europe and North Africa. He worked in pen and ink with wash, producing illustrations on a wide variety of subjects that reproduced well in the half-tone process. Apart from his World War I illustrations, he is best known for his imaginative reconstruction of 'Nebraska Man' in the *ILN* in 1922.

HARRIS, Herbert H. (fl. 1918–1940)

H. H. Harris, as he signed his work, was active from around 1918 to 1940 as an illustrator, cartoonist, poster designer and commercial artist. He is credited with devising the slogan 'Bovril prevents that sinking feeling' for his poster depicting a man in his pyjamas adrift at sea and bobbing on a Bovril jar. He designed further posters for Bovril, contributed to *Pan* magazine, *The Passing Show* and *The Bystander* and illustrated a number of children's books.

HIGGINS, Reginald Edward (1877–1933)

Reginald Higgins's distinctive and pleasing flat colours mark him out as member of the 'poster school' of artists. He studied at St John's Wood Art School and then the Royal Academy and produced a large number of stylish railway posters for LNER during the 1920s. Interestingly, Lewis Baumer also attended St John's Wood Art School and both men were keen exponents of 'the modern girl'; Higgins even exhibited a group of paintings called 'Some Modern Girls' at the Sporting Gallery in December 1925. He painted a number of illustrations for *The Bystander* and *The Tatler* during and after the war, always depicting women as independent, stylish and occasionally aloof. His magazine illustrations during World War I are dominated by women's roles, from drivers to canteen workers. His distinctive style was ideally suited to The Decorative Art Group, of which he was a member. Profiled in *The Studio* magazine, the group sought to banish from their schemes 'that third dimension, the illusion of which is created by the use of shadows.'

KIRCHNER, Raphael (1875–1917)

Raphael Kirchner was born in Vienna. His father, a skilled calligraphist, urged his son to take up a musical career and Kirchner attended the Conservatoire in Vienna for a time. From 1890 to 1894 he studied at the Vienna School of Art, and then at the Spezialschule fur Historienmalerei (Special School for Historical Painting). His early commercial work received critical praise and in 1897 his first set of postcards 'Wiener Typen' was published by Philipp & Kramer. He moved to Paris in 1900, after when he produced illustrations for books, posters, portraits (few of which survive), ceramics and a wide variety of magazines including *La Vie Parisienne* and *Lustige Blatter*. His paintings of slim, alluring women known as the 'Kirchner Girls' were hugely popular. During World War I, Kirchner was represented in Britain by the Bruton Galleries in London, and his work began to appear regularly in *The Sketch*. In 1915, Kirchner left Europe for New York where he continued to work, particularly on the decoration of the Century theatre on Broadway. He died on 2 August 1917 of appendicitis.

LEETE, Alfred Chew (1882–1933)

The son of a Northamptonshire farmer, Alfred Leete was born at Thorpe Achurch and educated at Weston-super-Mare Grammar School. He began work as a printer and had his first work accepted for *Punch* in 1905. Early in the war, he designed a cover for *London Opinion* magazine featuring Kitchener, which was adapted to become the iconic 'Your Country Needs You' recruitment poster. Leete also drew the infamous Schmidt the Spy, a humorous anti-German character.

LUNT, Wilmot (fl.1910–1925)

The son of a Warrington merchant, Wilmot Lunt attended Botelar Grammar School, where the art teacher recognised his talent. He spent some time at the Lancashire School of Art before earning a county scholarship to train at the Royal College of Art in Kensington and the Academie Julian in Paris. His original intention was to be a painter in oils, but the necessity of earning a living led him to turn to 'black and white' work. His first drawings to be published appeared in *The Idler* under the editorship of Robert Barr. He was soon working for most of the illustrated periodicals including *Punch*, *London Opinion*, *The Tatler*, *The Sketch* and *The Bystander*. According to a profile in *The Strand* magazine in 1916, he gave 'much of his time to cartoons, and has found pleasure in ridiculing the Hun and his methods'. Lunt spent most of his spare time touring the United Kingdom on a motorcycle and used these sightseeing trips as inspiration for many of his backdrops, although he maintained that for pictures on topical matters, he felt it necessary to visit towns. He and his wife lived a rather bucolic existence, living in a converted railway booking office in a village on the outskirts of London, where they grew vegetables and kept a brood of Leghorn hens.

MACDONALD, Alistair Kenneth (1879/80–1948)

Born in Buenos Aires, A. K. Macdonald's first published work was in *Longbow* magazine in 1898 and shortly afterwards he began to contribute to *Pearson's*. His typically Art Nouveau style from this period brought him commissions from Pears' and Lux soaps, brands to which his deft, charming style was eminently suited. His subjects were almost always female including his drawings for *The Tatler* during the World War I period (there is no record of whether he saw active service during the war). His work for *The Sketch* during the 1920s and 30s is rather risqué, but, executed in Macdonald's trademark delicate, pastel-hued style, it takes on an acceptable patina. His work also appeared frequently in *The Strand* during this period. A second marriage in 1926 to a fellow artist, Alice Helene Watson, 25 years his junior, seems to have seen Macdonald's erotic imagination in full flower. At the outbreak of World War II, Macdonald continued to contribute to *The Sketch*, most commonly illustrating a weekly recipe column.

MATANIA, Fortunino (1881–1963)

Fortunino Matania was born in Naples in 1881. His father Eduardo was a well-respected southern Italian artist who made illustrations for a number of high-grade Italian publications such as the popular *Illustrazione Italiana*. Judged a child prodigy, Fortunino worked in his father's studio and illustrated his first book at the tender age of 14 (editors seeing work signed by Fortunino refused to believe that he could be the artist, until he visited their offices and made drawings before their eyes). He then worked for *Illustrazione*, followed by a stint at *L'Illustration* in Paris as well as at *The Graphic*. During his long and prolific career, he produced thousands of illustrations. The apogee of his output was during World War I, when he completed countless paintings for *The Sphere*. He visited the Front on several occasions and his illustrations cover all aspects of the war from battle charges to entertainment behind the lines. Matania often used family members as models and one model, Ellen Jane Goldsack ('Goldie'), became Matania's second wife in 1960 when Matania was 79 years old. Matania was still working and producing illustrations with his customary skill and accuracy during World War II. In addition, he was able to indulge his love of history by writing as well as illustrating a long-running series in the *ILN* magazine, *Britannia & Eve*. Lately considered unfashionable, Fortunino Matania remains one of the most accomplished painters in the genre of illustrated realism. Work by his father, Eduardo, and his uncle, Ugo, also appears in this book.

McKIE, Helen (1889–1957)

Helen McKie attended Lambeth School of Art from 1910 to 1912. She worked as a staff artist for *The Bystander* from 1915 to 1929, and had work published in its sister paper *The Graphic* as well as *Pearson's*, *The London Magazine*, *The Royal Magazine* and *The Queen*. Well travelled, she spent time in France and Poland during World War I, specialising in drawing scenes and soldiers behind the lines. A Francophile, she spoke fluent French and delighted in drawing military uniforms, especially of French soldiers (she provided the illustrations for a deluxe edition of P. C. Wren's *Beau Geste*). Her cosmopolitanism continued after the war, when she would send back drawings for *The Bystander*'s annual Riviera number. She exhibited at the Paris Salon twice, and in London in 1919. She decorated two coaches for a Continental boat train for the Southern Railway in 1919, painted scenes to decorate the British Railway cross-channel ferry, *Brittany*, and also carried out some mural designs for the Ritz Hotel in London as well as Butlin's Holiday Camps.

MORROW, Edwin (fl.1903–1935)

Edwin Morrow, known as 'Eddie' to friends and fellow Sketch Club members, was born in Belfast, one of eight brothers, five of whom became artists. His elder brother George was art editor of *Punch* between 1932 and 1938, with Edwin also a regular contributor to the magazine. Another brother, Norman, illustrated the theatrical pages of *The Bystander* but died during World War I. Edwin contributed regularly to *The Bystander* and exhibited at the Royal Academy.

OAKLEY, Harold Lawrence (1882–1960)

Lawrence Oakley was born in York on 28 December 1882. His father was a chemist and alderman of the city. He attended the art schools of York, Leeds and the Royal College of Art in London. He also received his ARCA diploma in architecture in 1908, and spent a period travelling in 1909, financially aided by two scholarships. He taught art for London County

Council, then at Worcester Royal Grammar School from 1911 to 1912. After a spell in Holland in 1913, where he was part of a team of artists decorating the Peace Palace in the Hague, he held an exhibition at the Assembly Rooms in York which included a selection of well-received silhouettes. He opened his first studio in London in the Army & Navy department store, the success of which led him to decide on a career as a silhouettist. During the war he joined the 8th Yorkshire Regiment (the Green Howards) along with two of his brothers. He designed a successful recruiting poster, 'Think', for the army, a design which was subsequently adapted for the navy. He sent back charming cuttings to *The Bystander* depicting life in the trenches and behind the lines. He was wounded in 1916 and sent back to hospital in England. On returning to France he was appointed ADC to the Commanding Officer of the 32nd Division, Major General T. S. Lambert. After the war, Oakley returned to full-time silhouette art, dividing his time between portraiture, magazine and commercial work. He would set up temporary studios in London, Edinburgh and other places, and during the summer season worked from kiosks and booths in seaside towns. He was particularly fond of Llandudno. During a career that lasted four decades, Oakley cut literally tens of thousands of silhouettes, including numerous members of the royal family, writers, artists, sportsmen, entertainers and other prominent personalities.

OWEN, Will (1869–1957)

Born in Malta, the son of an engineer in the Royal Navy, Will Owen was first educated at the Mathematical School in Rochester and then studied at Lambeth School of Art. His work is similar in style to that of Tom Browne and John Hassall, using heavy outlines, and his full-page cartoons for *The Bystander* and *The Sketch* were highly popular. His collaboration with W. W. Jacobs, whom he met while working at the Post Office Savings Bank, prior to taking up illustration full time, lasted many years, with Owen illustrating Jacobs' novels and short stories for *The Strand* magazine. He also wrote his own stories, and eventually left illustration to work as a journalist at the *East Kent Mercury*. He was a prolific poster artist, the most famous of his work being the 'Bisto Kids' creation.

PEGRAM, Fred (1870–1937)

Fred Pegram was the cousin of H. M. and C. E. Brock and worked for a number of periodicals from the late 1880s onwards. He illustrated many short stories and had a unique style which used fine lines and gradations to suggest shading. Pegram also illustrated some memorable advertisements, notably for Kenilworth Cigarettes and Kodak, for whom Pegram devised the budding lady photographer in a striped dress known as the 'Kodak girl'.

REED, Edward Tennyson (1860–1933)

E. T. Reed was educated at Harrow School and regularly accompanied his father, who was the Admiralty's Designer of Warships and a Member of Parliament, to the House of Commons,

forming there his talent for political caricature. A friend of Edward Burne-Jones and Linley Sambourne, the latter recommended him to *Punch*, to which he first contributed in 1889. He was elected to the *Punch* table the following year, succeeding Harry Furniss as their parliamentary cartoonist in 1894. He is largely associated with *Punch*, but he also contributed a picture most weeks to *The Bystander* in the decade leading up to the outbreak of war and throughout World War I. He also drew for *The Bystander*'s sister magazine, *The Graphic*. Working mainly in pencil, few key figures of the day escaped his attention. King George V owned a caricature of himself by E. T. Reed.

REYNOLDS, Frank (1876–1953)

Born in London, the son of an artist, Frank Reynolds studied at Heatherley's School of Art and from the 1890s worked on the staff of both *The Illustrated London News* and *The Sketch* under the editorship of Keble Bell. Reynolds specialised in drawing 'types' – low lifes and street characters in the tradition of Phil May or Charles Keene, evident in series such as 'Peculiarly British Types' published in the *ILN* in 1910. He was a member of the London Sketch Club and was friendly with John Hassall, who advised him to move from pen and ink to pencil and crayon, allowing Reynolds to become more proficient in watercolour also. His illustrations for Dickens' novels in 1910–12 were a great success, with his characters afterwards used in advertising. He joined *Punch* in 1919 and succeeded F. H. Townsend as art editor from 1921 to 1931. He was still drawing during World War II, contributing a full-page cartoon to each issue of *The Sketch*. One of Reynolds's most famous drawings was for *Punch* during World War I, depicting a German family sitting around the breakfast table indulging in their 'morning hate'.

RITCHIE, Alick P. F. (1868–1938)

Alick P. F. Ritchie was a cartoonist and caricaturist who is best known for his contributions to *Vanity Fair* but also was published regularly in *The Bystander*. His portraits of celebrities of the day were constructed from a modern mix of lines, squares and circles, recalling the Futurist and Cubist movements. He was the subject of a short film in 1915 called *A Pencil and Alick P. F. Ritchie*, which featured Ritchie sketching various caricatures and wartime topics.

ROBINSON, Charles (1870–1937)

The elder brother of William Heath Robinson, Charles Robinson was born in Camden, North London, the son of Thomas Robinson, a magazine illustrator. He was apprenticed to the lithographers Waterlow & Son, and despite earning a place at the Royal Academy was unable to attend due to inadequate funds. He did however attend evening classes at the West London Art School and Heatherley's School of Art and worked from his father's studio in the Strand from 1892 as a freelance illustrator. In 1895, he illustrated Robert Louis Stevenson's *A Child's*

Garden of Verse with great success; he would go on to illustrate more than 100 books, mainly for children. Charles Robinson's freedom of style and air of romance mark him out as an artist of the 'Fairy School', along with Edmund Dulac and Arthur Rackham. His work shows clear influences of Aubrey Beardsley and Walter Crane, and his book illustration was supplemented by regular contributions to *The Sketch* and *The Bystander* during and especially after the war, the introduction of the four-colour process over lithography benefiting his delicate style greatly. Charles Robinson was, along with his brother, a popular member of the London Sketch Club, although with a somewhat conservative appearance he was often mistaken for a clerk rather than an artist. During the war, he enrolled as a member of the Volunteer Training Corps and at its disbandment had reached the rank of second lieutenant.

ROBINSON, William Heath (1872–1944)

William Heath Robinson, the youngest of three artist brothers, was born in Hornsey Rise, North London, in 1872. He studied at Islington School of Art and briefly at the Royal Academy and had initial hopes of becoming a landscape artist. However, he had a great talent for illustration and he established himself with his drawings for *The Poems of Edgar Allan Poe* in 1900. He also wrote and illustrated children's books of his own – *Uncle Lubin* in 1902 and *Bill the Minder* in 1912. But it was his talent for humorous drawing that was to establish him as one of the leading illustrators of the 20th century. Almost without a break, Heath Robinson was published in *The Sketch*, *The Tatler*, *The Illustrated Sporting and Dramatic News* and *The Bystander* from the Edwardian era right up until World War II. As well as book and magazine illustration he undertook numerous advertising commissions, notably for Hovis, Ransome's lawnmowers and Mackintosh toffees. His early drawings covered subjects as diverse as Eton schoolboys, 'British Sports and Pastimes', and predictive suggestions for German invasion techniques, while later illustrations are concerned chiefly with his machine drawings and inventions, for which he is justly famous. His hilarious illustrations during the Great War poked fun at both sides, although more often at German 'frightfulness'. One illustration published before the conflict, around the time Robert Blatchford was warning the British of the likelihood of war, showed German spies in a number of disguises watching the movements of a Boy Scout in Highgate Woods. The Germans did not quite understand the British sense of humour and reprinted the picture as a way of conveying British alarm at a possible German invasion! Having earned the title the 'Gadget King' through his ingenious ideas, Heath Robinson has the honour of being one of the few personalities from history to be named in the Oxford English Dictionary as the root of an adjective; the term 'Heath Robinson' is defined as relating to an overly complicated and often ramshackle construction, or anything unnecessarily convoluted. Heath Robinson's relationship with the *ILN* magazines went beyond a purely business one. In 1903, he married Josephine Latey, daughter of John Latey, assistant editor and briefly editor of *The Illustrated*

London News. His gentle wry humour, his unfailingly witty draughtsmanship and his endless stream of good ideas has deservedly made William Heath Robinson one of the best-loved illustrators of the 20th century.

ROUNTREE, HARRY (1878–1950)

Rountree, described as a 'genial humorist' in his *Times* obituary, was born and trained in New Zealand, and began his illustrative career designing jam jar labels. He joined the London Sketch Club three years after his arrival in London and was president from 1914–15. He was a particularly good friend of Harold Earnshaw who often partnered him at golf. He served as a captain with the Royal Engineers during the war.

SHEPPERSON, Claude Allin (1867–1921)

Claude Shepperson was born in Beckenham, Kent and initially trained as a barrister before studying at Heatherley's and in Paris. Highly respected by his artist peers, Shepperson was one of a number of well-known illustrators who worked as a tutor at Percy Bradshaw's Press Art School. Working in most media, Shepperson's pictures are a masterclass in elegance, grace and refinement, and scenes of high society, often featuring the 'Shepperson Girl', were a speciality. He contributed regularly to *The Tatler*, an ideal magazine to showcase his work.

STUDDY, George Ernest (1878–1948)

George Studdy was born in Devon on 23 June 1878, but he was educated at Dulwich College in south-east London. He studied art at evening classes and later spent a term at Frank Calderon's School of Animal Painting. Before taking up art full time, Studdy was apprenticed to an engineering firm, Thames Iron Works, and later worked as a stockbroker's clerk. His work was first regularly featured in *Comic Cuts*, leading to more commissions from other Fleet Street editors. He was first published by *The Tatler* in 1903 along with his brother Hubert, who wrote a story about a comic dog, which George illustrated – an inkling of what was to come. By 1912, Studdy was working regularly for *The Tatler*, *The Bystander*, *The Graphic*, *The Illustrated London News*, and most frequently, *The Sketch*. The majority of his World War I humorous drawings are from a home front perspective (Studdy was declared unfit for service), and although he was one of *The Sketch*'s most important artists, his real breakthrough came in 1922. For some years, Studdy had drawn a small, comic dog simply known as the 'Studdy dog'. However, readers clamoured for the dog to be named and so Bruce Ingram, editor of *The Sketch* and *ILN*, suggested the name 'Bonzo'. Bonzo, a little dog of indistinguishable breeding, with saucer-like eyes and a talent for getting into scrapes, proved to be an instant hit with adults and children alike. 'Bonzomania' continued through the 1920s and 30s with Bonzo reproduced in countless forms, from postcards to chocolate moulds and from inkwells to stuffed toys. The popularity of Bonzo brought Studdy a comfortable lifestyle and considerable fame, though he continued to lead a simple existence and was known to be exceptionally generous to friends and strangers alike. Studdy died of lung cancer in July 1948.

THORPE, James H. (1876–1949)

James H. Thorpe, who usually signed his work simply 'Thorpe', was born in Homerton, East London, and attended Bancroft's School in Woodford on a scholarship. Like Frank Reynolds, who was a good friend, he attended evening classes at Heatherley's School of Art and was able to leave his job as a schoolmaster to take up an artistic career in 1902. He was a regular contributor to *The Bystander*, especially of theatrical drawings. He served in the Artists' Rifles during World War I.

WATTS, Arthur (1883–1935)

Arthur Watts was the son of an army doctor, and was sent to school at Dulwich College, where academic endeavours came second to the doodles in his school exercise books. He went to Goldsmith's Institute in south-east London and then to the Slade School of Art, encouraged to pursue a career in art by his mother. He also studied at the Free Art School in Antwerp and then in Paris before returning to the Slade for a short time. In 1904, he began to be published in a number of publications, including *Pearson's*, *London Opinion*, *The Tatler*, *The Bystander*, and by 1912, *Punch*. In 1910, he bought his first boat, and began a lifelong love of sailing. He wrote and illustrated a series of articles for *Yachting World*, and in June 1913 set off on a three-week tour of the Dutch and Belgian coasts, an experience that would place him in good stead for his role in World War I, serving in the Coastal Motor Boats and Motor Launches in the Dover Patrol of the RNVR. As Lieutenant Commander, Watts led a smoke-screen flotilla at the battles of Zeebrugge and Ostend in 1918 and was awarded the DSO and mentioned in despatches. The resultant shellshock from his war experiences meant he was unable to return to drawing until 1921, when he was once more in *Punch*. Apart from his work for the *ILN* magazines and for *Punch*, Watts also produced four small drawings each week for 'Both Sides of the Microphone' in the *Radio Times* from 1928 to 1935. He illustrated E. M. Delafield's *Diary of a Provincial Lady* and drew some particularly humorous posters for London Transport. Arthur Watts was tragically killed at the age of 52 in an aeroplane crash on 20 July 1935, when returning from Italy.

WOOD, Clarence Lawson (1878–1957)

Born in Highgate, North London, in 1878, Lawson Wood (who disliked and never used his first name, Clarence) was the third generation of a family of artists. His father was Pinhorn Wood, the landscape painter, and his grandfather, L. J. Wood, had been a well-known artist of architectural subjects. Lawson Wood studied at Slade School of Fine Art, Heatherley's School of Art and Frank Calderon's School of Animal Painting before working for the book publisher Arthur Pearson as their principal artist from 1896 to 1902. He is best known for his humorous and immaculately executed animal paintings, particularly those of his wily orangutan 'Gran'pop', published in *The Sketch* during the 1930s. He was an astute businessman, retaining copyright in all his work, which was reproduced in annuals, postcards and even as plush toys. During World War I, Lawson Wood served as a balloonist with the Royal Flying Corps and was decorated by the French for his action over Vimy Ridge. He had a reputation as something of an eccentric recluse in later life, especially when he moved his lovely 15th-century manor house brick by brick from Sussex to Kent.

WOODVILLE, Richard Caton (1856–1927)

R. Caton Woodville (as he would sign his paintings) was born in London into an affluent family. His American father, who died before he was born, had been a painter of military subjects. Brought up in Russia and Germany, he studied art in Dusseldorf and Paris before settling in London in 1875, where he became a correspondent for the *ILN*. He covered the Russo-Turkish War of 1878, the Egyptian rebellion of 1882 and the Boer War (1899–1901) for the *ILN*, establishing a reputation for painting glamorous and dramatic action scenes, particularly cavalry charges. He is notorious for glossing over the more gory aspects of battle, but nevertheless excelled at painting the precise details of uniform and weaponry (he collected weapons and firearms during his travels and assembled them in his studio at Queen's Gate in London for visual reference). Admired by Vincent Van Gogh, Caton Woodville may be best known for his exciting battle scenes, but his pictures of the hardship in Ireland in 1880 demonstrates an artist with a wide range. His enthusiasm for the military extended beyond painting. He joined the Royal Berkshire Yeomanry Cavalry in 1879 and remained there until 1914, when he joined the National Reserve as a captain.

Index

Illustration titles are indexed by illustrator.